IMAGES
of America

THORNTON

IMAGES
of America

THORNTON

Tonja Dillon Castaneda

ARCADIA
PUBLISHING

Published by Arcadia Publishing
Charleston SC, Chicago IL, Portsmouth NH, San Francisco CA

Library of Congress Catalog Card Number: 2008928361

For all general information contact Arcadia Publishing at:
Telephone 843-853-2070
Fax 843-853-0044
E-mail sales@arcadiapublishing.com
For customer service and orders:
Toll-Free 1-888-313-2665

Visit us on the Internet at www.arcadiapublishing.com

This photograph really marked the end of an era as this farmland where wheat and alfalfa were grown was soon to be turned into Thornton's first homes. Pictured with farm equipment is pasture and rolling prairie, showing a true view of the rural landscape of this area before house building was started by Sam Hoffman in 1953. (Courtesy of Myrna Eppinger Wolfgang.)

CONTENTS

Acknowledgments   6

Foreword   7

Introduction   9

1.   The Town of Eastlake   11

2.   Early Homesteads and Schoolhouses   25

3.   One Man Has a Vision to Build Thornton   41

4.   Everyone Pitches in to Build a New Community   65

5.   Second Time a Charm for Incorporation   91

6.   Watching a City Grow and Surviving a Tornado   107

7.   Hitting a 50-Year Milestone and Still Going Strong   121

Bibliography   127

ACKNOWLEDGMENTS

A warm thank you goes to Thornton and Eastlake residents who shared family photographs and memories of their lives for the book. Thanks for letting your cherished photographs be published as a record of local history.

This book would also not be possible without assistance from the City of Thornton and access to Thornton's historical archives. Special thanks to the Thornton City Manager's Office, Cultural Division, and Communications Office.

Thank you to my husband, Ken, for encouraging me to write this book. To my children, Andrew and Kaitlin, I encourage you both to always reach for your dreams. I thank my parents, Jerry and Kaye Dillon, for their continued support. Thank you also to my Arcadia book editors Hannah Carney, Jerry Roberts, and Devon Weston for their sound advice.

Finally, I praise God for the creation of this book. My faith has guided me every step of the way, and I truly believe all things are possible with God.

City of Thornton Legal Disclaimer: The use of City of Thornton historical documents and photographs is in no way intended to represent or imply that the city has received or will receive revenue from the sale of the history book or in any way has sanctioned or is in any way a sponsor or associated with composition and publishing of the history book.

FOREWORD

This Thornton history book is dedicated to the first citizens of Thornton. These pioneers had the foresight to set the foundation and had a true commitment to their community. These people worked tirelessly in the first few years to form Thornton. For the hardships endured and all that followed, this book is a tribute to them.

Special thanks goes to the volunteer firemen and police officers who brought security and safety to Thornton in the early years. We also acknowledge those on the first Thornton City Council and all the people who followed in their footsteps to lead Thornton to where it is today.

—Oyer "Bill" Leary
First Thornton Mayor

—Gerald Carley
First Thornton City Councilman

Friendly colleagues Oyer "Bill" Leary, Thornton's first mayor, and Gerald Carley, a first Thornton city councilman, both moved to Thornton in 1954. Carley, who actively campaigned to incorporate Thornton, was a reporter for the *Thornton Thunder* and *Thornton Tribune* newspapers and Thornton Recreation Association (TRA) president. When running for mayor, Leary campaigned on the platform to construct a Thornton municipal building, which was dedicated in 1958. (Courtesy of the Carley family.)

INTRODUCTION

Life in the 1950s in Thornton was ideal in many ways. Nearly everyone was involved in caring for the community. Police served as volunteer crossing guards to protect schoolchildren, and Thornton's first doctors still made house calls. Children in Thornton grew up in a place where neighbors watched them and treated them as their own. Kids would play in the Hoffman Ditch when it rained under the watchful eyes of neighbors. Children rode bicycles to the Thornton Shopping Center, and if they were lucky, they had a nickel to buy ice cream at the Purity Creamery. Simple things made Thornton a good place to call home.

Just a few years earlier, it was the idea of one man to build "Colorado's newest city." Where before there had been farmland all around, a new town was being built north of Denver. Thornton was started in 1953 by Sam Hoffman, who seems to have worked a little magic to start a whole new community. He may have even had a touch of stardust on his fingertips. He invited Hollywood movie star Jane Russell to the opening of the Thornton model houses. Russell came to Thornton to decorate the model show homes and greet people coming to see the new housing development. Hoffman named the town after then Colorado governor Dan Thornton. Thornton was certainly off to an exciting start.

News of the new Thornton community was making headlines, and the home building business was booming. Hoffman's F&S Construction company was building up to 10 homes a day. Houses were being constructed in just three months time. A promise of "modern living" had people flocking to see the model homes. In many of the young families purchasing Hoffman homes, the husband was a World War II veteran who used the GI Bill to buy a brand-new brick home for around $10,000. The first family moved into Thornton in 1954, and many more followed.

Soon new residents of the community met their neighbors. People became friends, and their children played together. Neighbors often got together for block parties. They would gather to play cards, have coffee, and talk about the news of the day in Thornton.

Neighbors shared a common bond because most were young families. The husband was the provider who went to work, and the wife stayed home tending to the children and house. Most of the men were war veterans. They were happy to be here, living the American dream, and they were not afraid of doing hard work or volunteering time to improve their community. These first Thornton citizens worked together to build on Hoffman's vision.

At first, in Thornton, there were no street signs or phones, and it was dark at night because there were no streetlights. The main thoroughfare of Washington Street was a two-lane road because the Valley Highway, now Interstate 25, was not yet built. There was very little police or fire protection. The only transportation available at first was citizen's own cars. That would soon change as neighbors got organized to put into place the Thornton Fire and Police Departments, recreation facilities, and a form of community government.

When Hoffman started building Thornton, there was already another town, Eastlake, established to the north. The town of Eastlake today has ties to Thornton because it has been incorporated into the city's boundaries. However, when the first homes were built in Thornton, the two communities were separate.

Eastlake was founded about 50 years before Thornton. The town was started in about 1905, and a few years later, the Union Pacific Railroad was built through it. In the 1950s, Eastlake was a town supported by a rural community. Farmers had used the Eastlake railroad for decades, taking crops and livestock to market. Farms may have been spread out across the area, but these families were a tight-knit group of friends. The town of Eastlake was a hub where the rural community congregated to go to church, find out the news of the day, and socialize.

As this area grew, both of the communities of Thornton and Eastlake prospered, each with their own way of life. Another rural area south of Thornton, called Welby, would grow along with Thornton. In fact, the one thing that brought people in the area together was schools. Whether they lived in Thornton, Welby, or Eastlake, their children were educated together in community schools in Mapleton or Eastlake School Districts.

Schools were one of the main topics, as was police protection, when Thornton citizens decided to become an "incorporated" city. Community leaders petitioned for a citizen vote to become an official city by 1956. Many significant developments occurred in the 1950s, including opening a new Thornton City Hall in 1958. By 1963, Thornton had purchased its own water system. That foresight of early leaders is one of the reasons the city of Thornton is still able to grow and expand its boundaries.

As years went by and Thornton grew, progress marched north, eventually surrounding the town of Eastlake and going past its boundaries. Although it retains its own unique character, the town of Eastlake was annexed by the City of Thornton after a vote of Eastlake citizens in the 1990s. Thornton's boundaries now stretch from Eighty-fourth Avenue up to 168th Avenue with the city exceeding 34 square miles of land, including the town of Eastlake. Today around 118,000 people call Thornton home.

Two significant future events for Thornton promise continued change for the landscape. By 2015, Fastracks public transportation trains will run on railroad tracks from Denver to Thornton with a stop in Eastlake, just like trains stopped there 100 years ago. Also, in 2007, the City of Thornton updated a comprehensive plan that predicts population growth of up to 250,000 people calling Thornton home in the future.

This book provides a chronological, historical look back at this area from the past 100 years, including all the land that is now within the city of Thornton boundaries.

One

THE TOWN OF EASTLAKE

To look at the history that is the area of Thornton today takes a journey back 100 years to Eastlake. An 1899 map shows an area called East-Lake Farm owned by the Denver Land Company. Right after the turn of the 20th century, the town of Eastlake, Colorado, was founded by John Frank Church and Andrew Morrison Patten. Both men had an interest in bringing water from the mountains to irrigate farmland in Adams County, so they purchased 1,520 acres from Judge Charles Toll's estate around 1905.

They formed the Eastlake Investment Company, in which Church owned two-thirds and Patten owned one-third of the company. Three reservoirs in Eastlake held water to irrigate land subdivided into plots of 80- and 160-acre farms.

The Union Pacific Railroad was built by the fall of 1907 and daily service started on November 11, 1908. Farmers used rail to ship crops and livestock to market in Denver, and trains also took people to downtown. The town of Eastlake was officially platted by the Eastlake Investment Company on November 7, 1911.

The Eastlake State Bank opened in 1910, and both a dance hall and pool hall started operating. A man named William Hopkins established a lumber operation, a general store, bank, and drugstore in town. Founder Andrew Patten owned a hotel boardinghouse, and Dr. R. D. Elmore cared for the sick in Eastlake.

The Eastlake Post Office opened on June 8, 1912, and an Eastlake blacksmith shop operated in town. Around 1914, the Eastlake Grain Elevator opened, and the Farmers Co-Operative Elevator was built around 1920. That same year, Eastlake School opened for grades 1–12. The First Congregational Church of Eastlake was built around 1915, and Our Lady of Sorrows Catholic Church opened by 1917.

Eastlake was its own community for about 80 years before joining Thornton. In 1990, Eastlake residents voted for annexation by the City of Thornton to connect to city sewer service. The Eastlake Post Office still serves the 80614 Eastlake zip code, so Eastlake continues to truly retain an identity and charm all its own.

From Headquarters at Eastlake

This 1907 postcard from the town of Eastlake would have been one of the earlier photographs taken, as Eastlake was founded around 1905. This is one of the three reservoirs built to store irrigation water, which came from Clear Creek in the mountains. This card states it is from "Headquarters in Eastlake," which was located west of the Union Pacific Railroad tracks. (Courtesy of Andrew Patten Jr.)

The Eastlake Railroad Depot was on Lake Street east of the railroad tracks in the early 1900s. This photograph was taken around 1915 or 1916. The train depot served passenger train service to and from Denver and Greeley. It was retired by the railroad and moved from Eastlake in 1958. Eastlake will again provide passenger train service to Denver by 2015 as a rail transit corridor is built through Thornton, including a stop in Eastlake. (Courtesy of Mary Alice Bramming.)

A 1911 photograph shows the Eastlake Train Depot and the grain elevator along the railroad tracks. The house in the center was the first one built in Eastlake. In 1932, a baby girl named Doris Stockhaus was born in the railroad depot. Her parents were Otto and Bessie Stockhaus, and her dad worked for the railroad as part of the section crew that took care of the track. As part of his job, he was provided living quarters in the depot, which also housed a waiting room, office, and freight room. (Courtesy of Rod and Lorraine Snydal.)

The Union Pacific Railroad tracks built in 1907 brought farming business to Eastlake. At one time, there were two working grain elevators, a pickle factory, alfalfa mill, beet dump, and cattle corrals along the rail tracks in Eastlake. (Courtesy of Rod and Lorraine Snydal.)

John Frank Church was one of the founders of Eastlake around 1905. In the 1860s, Church's family homesteaded in Jefferson County on a site that became the Church Crossing Stage Stop on the Overland Stage Route. Frank Church and Andrew Patten purchased 1,520 acres, which became Eastlake. Their idea was to buy land to irrigate and then sell plots to people wanting to settle there and farm. (Courtesy of the Church-McKay family.)

These early settlers in Eastlake were colleagues as they shared common interests in Eastlake. Believed to be in this photograph are Andrew Patten, Frank Church, and K. G. Lambertson on a trip along the San Miguel River in Colorado during the 1930s. Patten and Church, who formed the Eastlake Investment Company, first met at a stockholder's meeting in 1904. (Courtesy of Bertha Lambertson.)

Andrew Morrison Patten, one of the founders of the town of Eastlake, purchased land with John Frank Church to create the Eastlake Investment Company. As manager of the company, Patten was well known, and he owned a hotel in town. He was said to be a fine fellow, and a handshake from Patten was more valid than any written contract. With a reputation as a real go-getter, it has been said about Patten that if he were alive today, he would be pioneering something. (Courtesy of Andrew Patten Jr.)

Early settler Kristian G. Lambertson is believed to have purchased one of the first plots of irrigated farmland in Eastlake. He bought 80 acres of land around 1913 from the Eastlake Investment Company after irrigation water was brought in. Lambertson emigrated from Denmark in 1884 to sail to America. At one time, Lambertson owned 248 acres of farmland. This 1910 postcard shows Lambertson with his wife, Frances, and son Lester when they visited Ireland. (Courtesy of the Lambertson family.)

15

This is a view of Lake Avenue in Eastlake around 1929. The front building is E. J. Snydal's store, and the two-story structure housed a dance hall and pool hall. The house on the northeast corner of Lake Avenue and Second Street was a hotel and boardinghouse. Migrant workers would come by train to stay at the hotel during farming season. (Courtesy of Rod and Lorraine Snydal.)

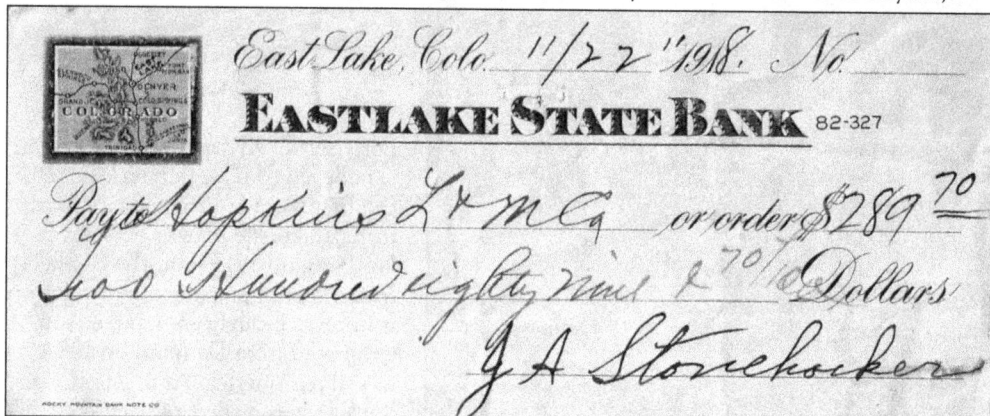

A 1918 Eastlake State Bank note is signed by J. A. "Jim" Stonehocker to the Hopkins Lumber and Mercantile in Eastlake for $289.70. The Eastlake State Bank was at the corner of Lake Avenue and First Street. The Stonehockers farmed land near 104th Avenue to 112th Avenue just west of where the Thornton Recreation Center is today. The Stonehockers also farmed on land that is now the Woodglenn subdivision. (Courtesy of Rod and Lorraine Snydal.)

16

Two little boys in Eastlake in the 1920s take time to stop and smell the flowers. The children are Kenneth Wayne Flint, age 3, and Lloyd Carroll Flint, 18 months old. The Eastlake Investment Company officially recorded Eastlake as a town on June 22, 1911, and created the streets, which still exist today. (Courtesy of Ben Ginther Jr.)

Eastlake was covered with a huge snowfall sometime in the 1920s. Pictured here is E. J. Snydal shoveling snow from the sidewalk in front of his store in Eastlake after the blizzard. The snowfall would have brought people out to ice skate on Lambertson's Lake. (Courtesy of Rod and Lorraine Snydal.)

Four young ladies spend time together in front of the Eastlake School. When Eastlake School opened in 1920 for grades 1 through 12, there were two teachers. In 1954, Eastlake was teaching grades one through five, as students in grades six through nine went to Westlake School. High school students went to Adams City High School, Westminster High School, or Brighton High School. (Courtesy of Rod and Lorraine Snydal.)

Some of the most memorable Eastlake stories tell about happenings in the 1920s. A fire broke out in Eastlake in 1926, as pictured, burning down the grocery store and a machine shed. The dance hall and pool hall were also destroyed in the suspected arson fire. The year before, in 1925, the Eastlake State Bank was robbed. When the getaway car failed to start, the thieves took off carrying $13,000, but locals captured them. (Courtesy of Rod and Lorraine Snydal.)

Pictured here is Lake Avenue in the late 1930s or early 1940s in the town of Eastlake. Bob and Louise Estrabrook and daughter Ethel are in front of their 1937 Plymouth. The car is parked in front of their barbershop, pool hall, and ice-cream parlor on Lake Avenue. Today the town of Eastlake is bounded by 124th and 128th Avenues, railroad tracks to the west, and York Street to the east. (Courtesy of Rod and Lorraine Snydal.)

This photograph shows the drugstore in Eastlake. Some may remember the sound of the bell on the drugstore door that rang when the door was opened. At one time, the back part of the drugstore housed the Eastlake Post Office. A few years later, the post office was moved across the street. Here store owner James Elmore works in the drugstore during the 1950s. (Courtesy of Myrna Eppinger Wolfgang.)

These are all the students that attended Eastlake School for the 1926–1927 school year. The photograph was taken in front of the Eastlake School. Adams 12, formed in 1951 with the consolidation of the following rural school districts: Hutchinson District No. 20, Westlake District No. 34, and parts of Burn Lee No. 6, Welby No. 26, and Eastlake No. 12. (Courtesy of Rod and Lorraine Snydal.)

Eastlake School opened for students in grades 1–12 in 1920. Here is a photograph of the Eastlake School with school buses parked in front around 1926. Mr. and Mrs. Sam Mundell, the custodians at the school, drove the buses and tended the playground. (Courtesy of John Lauridson.)

A school bus from the Eastlake Consolidated School District No. 12 picks up students to take them to Eastlake School. Pictured are Edwin (left), Elsie (standing on the bus step), and Otis Whytal being picked up from their farm near 118th Avenue and Huron Street in the 1920s. (Courtesy of Glen Lambertson.)

This 1937 Eastlake School photograph shows student athletes and the various sports they played. Eastlake students played Brighton and Westminster in baseball, basketball, boxing, and track and field. The bamboo poles the boys are holding were used for the pole vault event. In the back, the fire escape chute that Eastlake School students would slide down during fire drills can be seen. (Courtesy of Elizabeth Marion Hutchison.)

Pictured are the 1931 first- and second-grade classrooms at Eastlake School. A few of the students who can be identified are Walter Stonehocker (third row, second from right), Ben Ginther (third row, third from left), and John Lauridson (holding the sign in the front). (Courtesy of Ben Ginther Jr.)

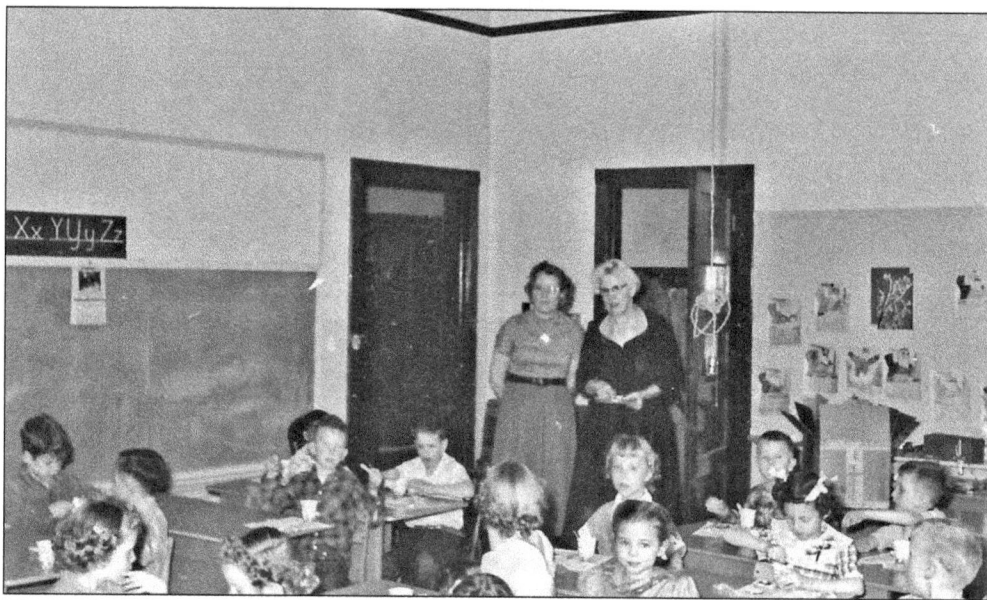

This is a first-grade classroom at the Eastlake School in 1955. First-grade teacher Mrs. Schaffer is on the right and room mother Alice Bramming is on the left. (Courtesy of Mary Alice Bramming.)

The Eastlake Congregational Church was organized more than 90 years ago. The church began in 1914 when Sunday evening services were held in a room over the Eastlake pool hall, which is now the Eastlake Inn. In October 1914, Sunday school was started in the home of Mrs. W. A. Twombley, who lived in a boxcar. (Courtesy of Eastlake Congregational Church.)

Members of the Eastlake Congregational Church are coming out of church in the 1950s. The church was incorporated on January 11, 1915, with 26 charter members. On June 13, 1915, the first worship service was held in the church even though the windows were not yet installed. William Kortum is wearing the hat, and his wife, Sophie Kortum, is coming out of the church behind him. (Courtesy of Eastlake Congregational Church.)

Eastlake's Our Lady of Sorrows Mission Catholic Church was dedicated on November 13, 1917. By the 1950s, a gas furnace replaced coal heat and indoor plumbing was installed. Members of the 1950 First Communion class are, from left to right, (first row) Lee Koleski and unidentified; (second row) Jim Lauridson and Beverly Fonay; (third row) Joanne Kalcevich, Sharon Koleski, Frances Shafer, and Mary Alice Bramming; (fourth row) Sister Marina, Fr. Herbert Banigan, and an unidentified nun. (Courtesy of Mary Alice Bramming.)

Art Eppinger stands in the yard of his Eastlake home on Lake Avenue in the 1950s. Art and his wife, Dorothy, lived in the Eastlake house. They sold property at Eighty-eighth Avenue and Washington Street in 1952 to Thornton land developer Sam Hoffman, who built the first houses in Thornton. Our Lady of Sorrows Catholic Church is in the background. (Courtesy of Myrna Eppinger Wolfgang.)

Two

EARLY HOMESTEADS AND SCHOOLHOUSES

In the 1940s, Eastlake farmers were still driving cattle and sheep to market across the land that is Thornton today. Herds were moved from homesteads to the Eastlake railroad.

Animals were held in stock pens near the tracks until they were loaded on trains taking them to be sold in Denver, Nebraska, and beyond. Their destination depended on regional commodity market prices. Harvested crops were also shipped by rail.

Farmers first emigrated here from Europe in the 1800s looking to prosper in America. They traveled west and worked as farm hands to earn money to purchase their own farms, or they homesteaded in the area.

They toiled over the soil to feed their families and pay their debts. They planted wheat, barley, and labor-intensive sugar beet crops. They raised cattle and sheep and ran dairy operations.

These were the first settlers to this part of Adams County, which has become Thornton. Some early citizens were water pioneers, digging canals to irrigate the land.

Farmers were always pursuing new machinery to improve farming methods. They flooded land to irrigate crops, used threshing machines to harvest wheat, and used mules to do heavy labor.

Farm families were self-sufficient and loved the land. Farmer's children attended one-room schoolhouses at the turn of the 20th century. By 1887, there were organized school districts in the area.

These farmers were dedicated to their way of life. Neighbors in rural communities may have lived farther apart, but they relied greatly on each other. They had picnics at different homesteads on Sunday afternoons. In the 1930s and 1940s, farmers met at the Riverdale Grange at 100th Avenue and Riverdale Road for Farm Association meetings, square dances, and socials.

But changes were coming in the decades that brought modernization to farming. Over time, more and more houses dotted the landscape as the area became suburbanized.

The strong rural values and commitment to farm life ran deep with families who had sown the land for more than 100 years. As more people moved to this area, an entire way of life in the farming community would be changed forever.

Denmark immigrant Fred Bramming came to America in 1904 and bought an 80-acre farm in 1915 at the corner of 128th Avenue and Holly Street. In this photograph, mules are pulling a cart to pick up bundles of wheat on the farm in the 1930s. Mules were used for their strength and endurance. The farmers had tractors by then but still used animals for some of the manual farm labor. (Courtesy of Mary Alice Bramming.)

By 1940, the Bramming farm had grown to 200 acres and was surrounded by 120th Avenue, Holly Street, and 128th Avenue. This photograph shows the process of threshing wheat during a 1930s harvest. A threshing machine separated the grains of wheat from the straw as it harvested the grain. Fred and Maude Bramming farmed this area and raised three boys, Fred, Henry, and Ed, who grew up to farm this land. (Courtesy of Mary Alice Bramming.)

Eastlake farmers operated their farms the same way their fathers and grandfathers did going back to the turn of the century in the 1900s. However, they were always pursuing modernized machinery and new agricultural methods. This late 1940s photograph on the Bramming farm shows a combine that both cut and threshed the grain. (Courtesy of Mary Alice Bramming.)

Before hay balers, farmers used a process called haying to make stacks of hay to feed to livestock. In this June 1944 photograph, a farmer drives a tractor to stack hay. (Courtesy of Mary Alice Bramming.)

Here at the Bramming brothers farm are Fred and youngster Mary Alice Bramming, both inside the truck, and Henry Bramming during the sugar beet harvest in October 1945. The harvest took place in the Eastlake area that is today at about 128th Avenue and Holly Street. (Courtesy of Mary Alice Bramming.)

Farmers grew wheat, alfalfa, barley, corn, and sugar beets in the area that has become Thornton. This photograph shows the labor-intensive sugar beets that were harvested to be processed and sold. The tops of the sugar beets were cut off and fed to livestock on the farms. Henry Bramming is on his way to the sugar beet dump at Eastlake with sugar beets that were harvested in the late 1930s. They would be put on railcars and taken to the sugar factory in Brighton. (Courtesy of Mary Alice Bramming.)

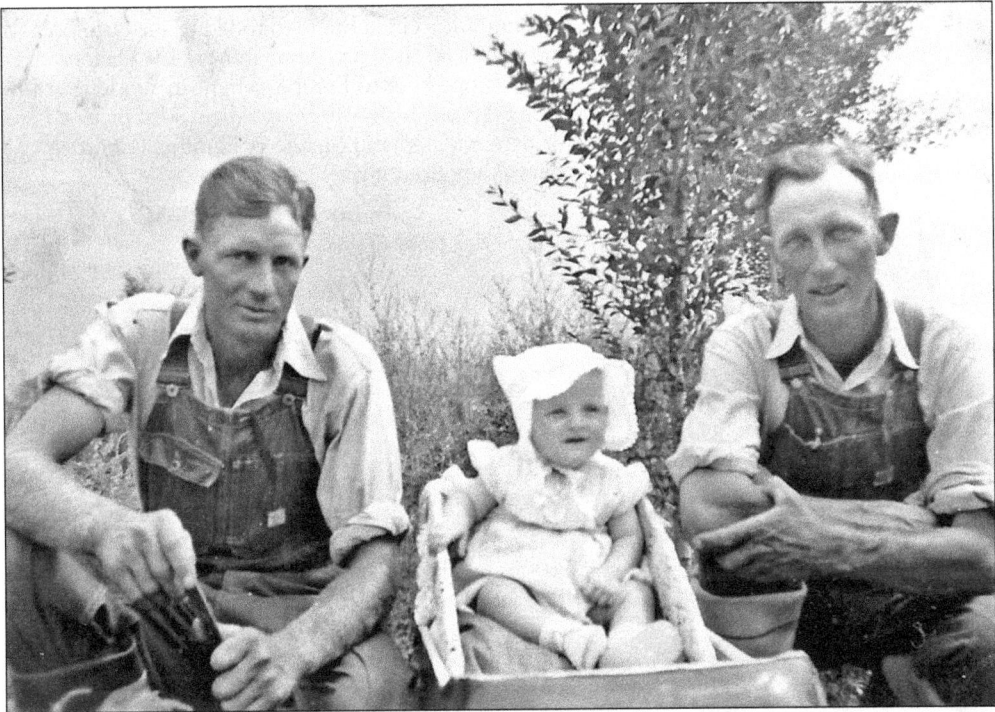

In summer 1943, Henry Bramming and his brother Fred Bramming take a break from irrigating the farm to sit by six-month-old baby Mary Alice Bramming, dressed up in a bonnet. When Eastlake farmers were ready to irrigate crops, they told a ditch tender to send water down a series of ditches from the Eastlake reservoirs and into their fields. The irrigation watershed came from the Mount Evans area down Clear Creek to the Highland Canal and into another ditch to the lake at Eastlake. (Courtesy of Mary Alice Bramming.)

Farmers in this area raised cattle and sheep on local farms. Shown here is farmer Ed Bramming with sheep in the pens on the Bramming farm, which is now on the east side of Thornton. (Courtesy of Mary Alice Bramming.)

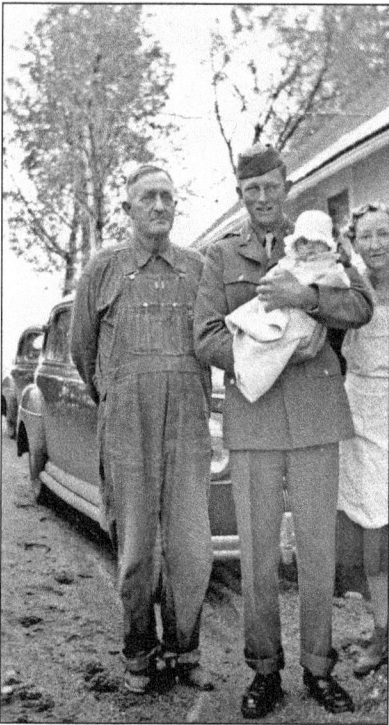

Ed Bramming came home to the Eastlake farm on furlough from the U.S. Army in May 1943 before being shipped out to Europe to fight in World Ward II. Here Ed holds his niece Mary Alice. Also pictured are his parents, Fred and Maude Bramming. (Courtesy of Mary Alice Bramming.)

The aerial photograph shows the Bramming farm in 1948 just west of Holly Street and 120th Avenue. The home place, horse and cattle barn, chicken house, garage, wooden granary, and two-room farmhand quarters can all be seen in the photograph. (Courtesy of Mary Alice Bramming.)

The Lambertson farm, still located at Washington Street and 100th Avenue, was purchased by K. G. Lambertson. His son Kristian Lambertson and wife, Bertha, took over the 80-acre farm in 1934 and farmed corn, alfalfa, wheat, and sugar beets. The barn on the property remains part of the Thornton landscape today, as houses in the Lambertson Lakes subdivision are now built around it. (Courtesy of City of Thornton Archives.)

Lester Lambertson, pictured in 1946 with his sons LeRoy and Glen, uses a combine to cut grain in the fields on his farm in Eastlake, near 124th Avenue and Claude Court. (Courtesy of Glen Lambertson.)

Lee and Shirley Carlson farmed 156 acres on 100th Avenue, between Washington Street and Colorado Boulevard, for decades. Lee Carlson was one of seven children born to area farmers Harry Frederick and Elsa Carlson. Earlier, in the 1920s, the Carlsons farmed land at the southeast corner of Eighty-fourth Avenue and the Valley Highway and the area where Skyview High School is today. Pictured from left to right are Stanley Carlson, Elsa Carlson holding Leona Carlson, family friend John Johnson holding Lee Carlson, Harry Carlson Jr., Harry Carlson Sr., and Gunnar Carlson, who was visiting from Sweden. (Courtesy of the Carlson family.)

The Ginther family came from Russia in 1889 and purchased a 320-acre farm at the southwest corner 128th Avenue and Holly Street by 1902. Adam Ginther married the former Fannie Bell, and by 1917, they had built a 16-room house at 130th Avenue and Holly Street. Pictured here is their son Ben Ginther, who took over the farm, as he holds his baby daughter Virginia in 1925. (Courtesy of Ben Ginther Jr.)

Youngsters find a swimming hole to cool off in during the summer of 1938. Neighboring farm children, including the Ginthers and the Cunnings, would swim together in the pond on sunny days on the Cunning farm at the southeast corner of 128th Avenue and Colorado Boulevard. (Courtesy of Ben Ginther Jr.)

Ben Ginther Jr. and Virginia Ginther dressed warmly on a cold winter day on the Ginther farm at 128th Avenue and Holly Street in the 1930s. (Courtesy of Ben Ginther Jr.)

Charles "C. E." and Mary Francis Luker are pictured on their farm with grains, either barley or oats, which would be put into a threshing machine during the harvest. Charles Luker gained notoriety in 1932 when he met U.S. presidential candidate Franklin Roosevelt in Denver. Luker appealed to Roosevelt to help farmers when he was about to lose the farm. Four years later, Luker (of Eastlake) met Roosevelt again, and he gave the president credit for helping to save his farm and his prosperity, as he yielded a $16,000 wheat crop. (Courtesy of the Hobbs family.)

Stacking hay on the Luker farm in Eastlake provided food for livestock throughout the winter months. Turkeys, seen here roaming the farm, were raised there and sold to downtown Denver hotels for holiday meals. (Courtesy of the Hobbs family.)

34

Mary Francis Luker gathers corn stalks to feed the pigs on the farm in Eastlake in the late 1930s or early 1940s. The pigs would eat the ears of corn. The Luker's 80-acre farm was located off 128th Avenue east of Colorado Boulevard. (Courtesy of the Hobbs family.)

Italian immigrants Concetta and Frank Mazzotti, pictured in the front row, first farmed 5 acres in the late 1800s where the Village Inn near Eighty-fourth Avenue and Interstate 25 is now in Thornton. The family farm moved to the Welby area around 1901 to continue growing vegetables. Here the Mazzotti family shows some of the vegetables they grew in 1933. Also pictured from left to right are (second row) Joe and George Mazzotti; (third row) Frank Gaccetta and Fred Mazzotti. (Courtesy of George Mazzotti.)

This 1935 photograph shows Frank Mazzotti on his horse, named Prince, at the family farmstead located at 1601 East Seventy-third Avenue in Welby. Also pictured are, from left to right, Fred Mazzotti, Gus Molinaro, and George Mazzotti. The Mazzotti boys' grandfather bought land to farm in Welby around 1901. (Courtesy of George Mazzotti.)

Pictured here in Welby in 1944 are, from left to right, (front) cousins Alice Gaccetta Nichol and Elaine Gaccetta Valente with (back) their grandmother Theresa Gaccetta and Concetta Mazzotti. Both girls grew up to run for public office, and both have served as an Adams County commissioner. (Courtesy of George Mazzotti.)

The Block Street School was located on the northwest corner of 120th Avenue and Colorado Boulevard. The school, which was built in 1907, taught grades one through eight. (Courtesy of John Lauridson.)

This photograph, taken on October 16, 1919, shows a group of classmates at the Block Street School, formerly in School District No. 4. Pictured here in no particular order are teacher Margaret Robertson and students Marian Esther Flint, Lorene Williams, Faye Farmer, Ruth Johnson, Margaret and Thadur Gallagher, Tommy Cundall, Lola Luker, Ronald Cundall, Paul Phillips, and Clara Johnson. Others are Carl Lauridson, Clarence Lauridson, Jack Orrison, Max Cundall, Johnnie Travers, and Annie Travers. (Courtesy of Ben Ginther Jr.)

The Washington School educated students in grades one through eight in the former District No. 16, which was consolidated into the Mapleton School District No. 1 in 1954. This photograph shows classmates from the Washington School around 1930. George Mazzotti (front row, third from left) is in the second grade in this photograph. Mazzotti grew up to become the first paid fire chief of the North Washington Fire Protection District in 1968. (Courtesy of George Mazzotti.)

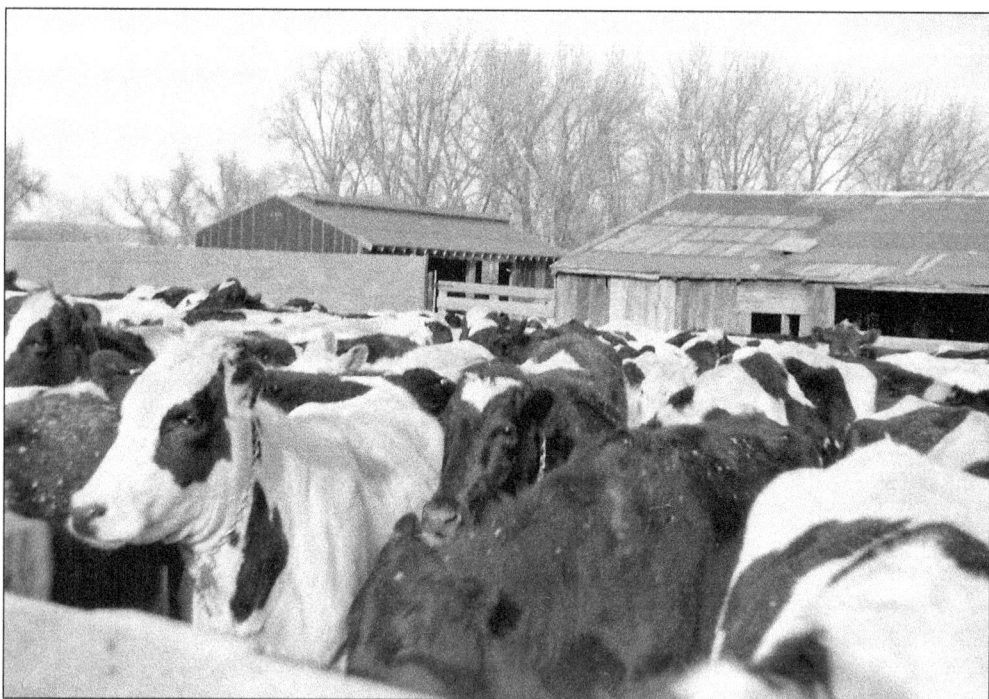

Karl's Farm Dairy, at 120th Avenue between Irma Drive and Race Street, remains a part of the Eastlake community. The dairy was purchased by C. R. "Bud" and Fern Hinkhouse in 1947 from Karl and Alys Obluda, who had been operating the dairy since the 1930s. This photograph was taken after the Hinkhouse family purchased the dairy. (Courtesy of Karl's Farm Dairy.)

The Hinkhouse family has operated Karl's Farm Dairy on 59 acres north of 120th Avenue since 1947. The dairy operates a creamery on the site and was known for years for having the richest whipping cream around. In this photograph, Robert Miskol bottles milk at Karl's Farm Dairy in the mid-1960s. He has worked at the dairy since 1959. (Courtesy of Karl's Farm Dairy.)

In 1947, Karl's Farm Dairy had 18 cows and made one milk route delivery every other day. By 1975, the dairy had grown to 400 cows and 18 milk routes. Here owners Fern and C. R. "Bud" Hinkhouse stand on the Karl's Farm Dairy property in 1954, with a milk truck in the background. Family owned and operated for three generations, Karl's Farm Dairy still sells milk and other Colorado products out of its country store on 120th Avenue. (Courtesy of Karl's Farm Dairy.)

Pictured in the 1940s, the Riverdale Grange Hall, located at 100th Avenue and Riverdale Road, was built around 1925. The farmers in the area belonged to the Grange for educational and social opportunities as well as insurance. By the 1950s, Thornton community groups had events at the Grange hall. In fact, the Thornton Fire Department held a 1967 New Year's Eve party there, before the building burned down in later years. (Courtesy of Ed Hubbell.)

Going to square dances at the Riverdale Grange Hall on Saturday nights was a popular thing to do in the 1940s. Horseshoe-throwing team contests, plays, and vaudeville shows were also held at the Grange hall. Pictured here is a square-dance group in front of the Riverdale Grange Hall. Harold and Ruth Hubbell are seen at far left. (Courtesy of Ed Hubbell.)

Three

ONE MAN HAS A VISION TO BUILD THORNTON

A new era had begun in a place called Thornton, when two shovels of dirt were turned in a farm field on April 2, 1953. That was when F&S Construction Company held a ceremony to start a construction project for 5,000 new homes. The ceremony was held off North Washington Street about 7 miles north of downtown Denver.

This land was previously owned by Art Eppinger, whose family had farmed for decades in Adams County. The Eppingers sold 640 acres near East Eighty-eighth Avenue and North Washington Street to Sam Hoffman for the housing project.

A few weeks after the ceremony, the model homes were already constructed and open for tours. A grand opening for the new Hoffman Homes was held on April 19, 1953, and thousands of people attended. Movie star Jane Russell came to Thornton to decorate the model homes and greet people at the new housing development.

Thornton was planned to have housing, parks, schools, and a shopping district all on 1,500 acres. The new community would also include churches, a fire station, and a community swimming pool. The brochure for Hoffman Homes touted "modern" brick homes and a clothesline in every backyard, and every house had central heating and large closets.

Hoffman Homes offered three model homes to buyers. The Arden model was a two-bedroom, one-bath home totaling 850 square feet for $8,350. The Ashley model was 1,150 square feet, with three bedrooms and one-and-a-half baths for $9,850. A third model, called the Clayton, had three bedrooms, one-and-a-half bathrooms, a dining room, and 1,170 square feet for $10,250.

By the next year, people started moving into the new community. The first families arrived in Thornton on January 31, 1954. Neighbors soon became friends, and they joined to make Thornton a place people were proud to call home. Whether it was volunteering to be a fireman or police officer or organizing the Thornton Junior Women's Club, everyone very quickly got involved in the spirit of starting a new town.

Colorado governor Dan Thornton was in office in the 1950s when the community of Thornton was built. Thornton developer Sam Hoffman decided to name the new community after Dan Thornton, who served as Colorado governor from 1951 to 1955. Governor Thornton made a visit to Thornton for the grand opening in 1953. (Courtesy Colorado State Archives.)

In 1952, the land that was to become the first housing development in Thornton was still prairie where cattle grazed. Farmer Art Eppinger and his wife, Dorothy, sold 640 acres at Eighty-eighth Avenue and Washington Street to developer Sam Hoffman for a housing construction project. Pictured are Dorothy Eppinger and her daughter Myrna on the farm that later became the first of the Hoffman Homes. Both Dorothy and Myrna have streets named after them in Thornton. (Courtesy of Myrna Eppinger Wolfgang.)

Thornton builder Sam Hoffman, center, stands with William and Sophie Kortum during the model show homes grand opening. Right behind them, people are lined up to tour the three model homes in Thornton in April 1953. (Courtesy of Myrna Eppinger Wolfgang.)

A Hoffman Homes brochure shows that a house in Thornton could be purchased for around $10,000 in 1953. According to a sales brochure, all Hoffman homes offered "central heating, copper lifetime plumbing, inside storage, screened windows and doors, large closets in bedrooms, and clothes line poles." (Courtesy of City of Thornton Archives.)

Pictured are, from left to right, Roy Bisterfeldt of the Farm and Ranch Exchange, builder Sam Hoffman, and landowner Art Eppinger standing at the model homes in Thornton. The Hoffman Homes sales brochure promised home buyers a future community with a city hall, fire station, parks, swimming pool, schools, churches, water and disposal plants, shopping center, and playgrounds. (Courtesy of City of Thornton Archives.)

A sign near the construction of the Hoffman Homes development entices people to think about buying a new home. This sign tells about "The Ashley" home, with three bedrooms, which could be purchased for $9,850. (Courtesy of the Carley family.)

Thornton home builder Sam Hoffman is pictured with Hollywood actress Jane Russell in 1953 at the grand opening for the Hoffman model homes. Hoffman invited the movie star to decide upon the interior decorating for two of the model homes since her brothers worked construction with Hoffman. Russell Boulevard in Thornton is named after the movie star. Russell's most memorable film roles include *The Paleface* in 1948 and *Gentlemen Prefer Blondes* in 1953. (Courtesy of City of Thornton Archives.)

The Father and Son Construction Company soon had construction of new Thornton homes underway. Hoffman's construction company put in roads, but many times after new homeowners had already moved into their houses. (Courtesy Myrna Eppinger Wolfgang.)

On opening day for the model homes at the new Hoffman Homes development in Thornton, thousands came out to tour the show homes. The Hoffman home marketing brochure read, "This

planned community brings the ultimate in modern design to those who will become the first citizens of this newest community of Hoffman Homes." (Courtesy of Myrna Eppinger Wolfgang.)

This photograph was taken in 1953 at the Hoffman model show homes opening. Pictured from left to right are F&S decorator Laura Gabrielson, actress Jane Russell, Art Eppinger, Sam Hoffman, Dorothy Eppinger, and daughter Myrna Eppinger in front. The Eppinger family sold the property to Hoffman for his proposed 5,000-home project. These houses became the start of the city of Thornton. (Courtesy of Myrna Eppinger Wolfgang.)

F&S Construction president Sam Hoffman decided to build a new town called Thornton in 1952. He purchased land from Adams County couple Art and Dorothy Eppinger at Washington Street north of Eighty-eighth Avenue. Pictured from left to right are the Eppingers, Hoffman, Mr. Goldberg, actress Jane Russell, and Mrs. Goldberg in April 1953. The group took time out from the grand opening of the Hoffman show homes to eat at Ciancio's Welby Tavern on York Street in Welby. (Courtesy of Myrna Eppinger Wolfgang.)

In November 1953, there were still no paved roads or trees in the Hoffman Homes development in Thornton. In the photograph, much of the landscape is still bare because houses were still under construction. (Courtesy of Patrick Surrena.)

Hoffman homes were under construction in 1953, and the first residents of Thornton moved into their new homes in 1954. This is Clarkson Street, where the first row of houses was built. The bulldozer is grading the alley between Clarkson and Ogden Streets just prior to paving the streets and other alleys. (Courtesy of Patrick Surrena.)

When Thornton's first builder announced his plans to build a new city called Thornton, there was nothing but farmland in the area about 7 miles north of Denver. As the first homes are built on the landscape, the rolling prairie surrounding the new houses can be seen in this picture. (Courtesy of the Carley family.)

Looking south down Clarkson Street in June 1954 with Hoffman model homes in the background, this photograph, taken from the Surrena family home, shows next-door neighbors Ed and Beverly Brennan in front of their home. (Courtesy of Patrick Surrena.)

By January 1954, the houses were starting to be framed. The house the Carley family moved into is seen here under construction on Oak Place. Gerald and Jo Carley were very active in the Thornton community. Gerald Carley served on the inaugural Thornton City Council, and both were writers for the *Thornton Thunder* and *Thornton Tribune* newspapers. (Courtesy of the Carley family.)

In 1953 and 1954, the Hoffman Homes development was bustling with construction activity as builders put up new brick houses. Here many workers build homes in Thornton, and the image shows what the general work area looked like as the houses were built. (Courtesy of the Carley family.)

Gerald and Joan Edgar moved to their Hoffman home on Clayton Street on July 5, 1956. They took photographs while their home was under construction, so the next three pictures show the progression of the house being built in about a six-week period. Here Joan Edgar stands in front of the concrete foundation for her house on May 20, 1956. (Courtesy of Joan Edgar.)

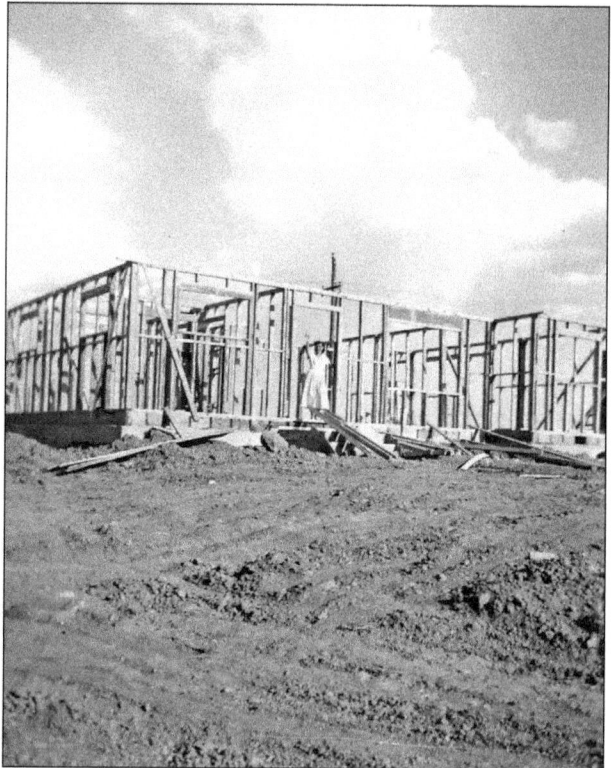

The second photograph in the series shows Joan Edgar standing in front of her brand-new Hoffman home under construction on June 8, 1956. This picture was taken looking toward the east to the next street over, Ciancio Street. (Courtesy of Joan Edgar.)

The Edgar house is almost finished by June 17, 1956, as it looks like contractors are ready to put the brick on the house at 9300 Clayton Street. When completed, every Hoffman home came with a trash incinerator outside. (Courtesy of Joan Edgar.)

The Edgar home on Clayton Street was under construction for just seven weeks. F&S Construction Company worked from May 6 through June 24 building the home. This photograph was taken on June 24, 1956, and the family moved in two weeks later. (Courtesy of Joan Edgar.)

Gerald and Jo Carley would visit the construction site every week when their home was under construction. Here Jo Carley and her boys, Vince and Scott, visit the construction site in 1954. (Courtesy of the Carley family.)

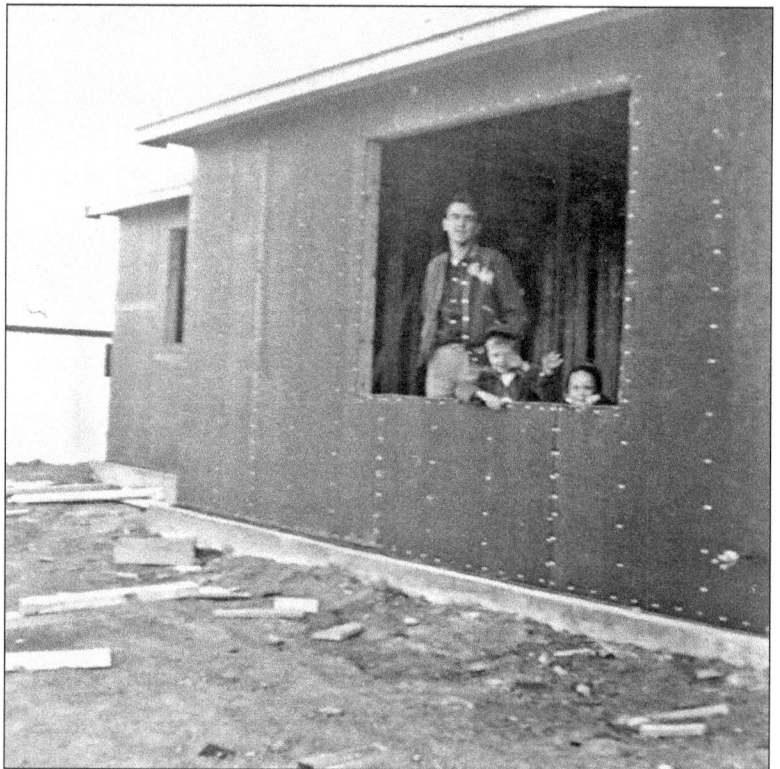

This picture shows Gerald Carley with his boys, Scott and Vince, inside their house under construction. The Carleys bought their house, an Ashley model, in May 1953 and moved into the house on Oak Place in March 1954. Home buyers of Hoffman Homes were mostly military veterans who were able to purchase a house for around $10,000. (Courtesy of the Carley family.)

Once people moved into their new homes, there was still much work to do. Here Gerald Carley uses a wheelbarrow to put in the front yard and a driveway at his house on Oak Place. Homeowners had to plant grass in their own yards, but neighbors usually helped each other with a great spirit of friendliness and cooperation. (Courtesy of the Carley family.)

Early on, Thornton citizens got to know their neighbors well. They held block parties, outdoor barbecues, and holiday celebrations. In fact, it was common for neighbors to go from house to house for impromptu gatherings to socialize. Here neighbors enjoy a get-together with lots of laughter and good food. (Courtesy of the Carley family.)

Oscar Hill, Thornton's first police chief, is pictured in the back row (far left) with friends Verne (center) and Mary Eiserman in the Hill home on Hoffman Way in Thornton in June 1960. In the front row are Nan Hill (left), Oscar Hill's daughter, and her friend Ruth Brent. (Courtesy of Oscar H. Hill family.)

Pictured here from left to right are Imogene Tarver, the first librarian at Meritt Hutton Junior-Senior High School as well as the business education teacher; Willis Tarver, the first principal of Meritt Hutton Junior-Senior High School; Tarby Tarver; and Oscar Hill. Katie Hill was also at the dinner, as was her daughter Nan. (Courtesy of Oscar H. Hill family.)

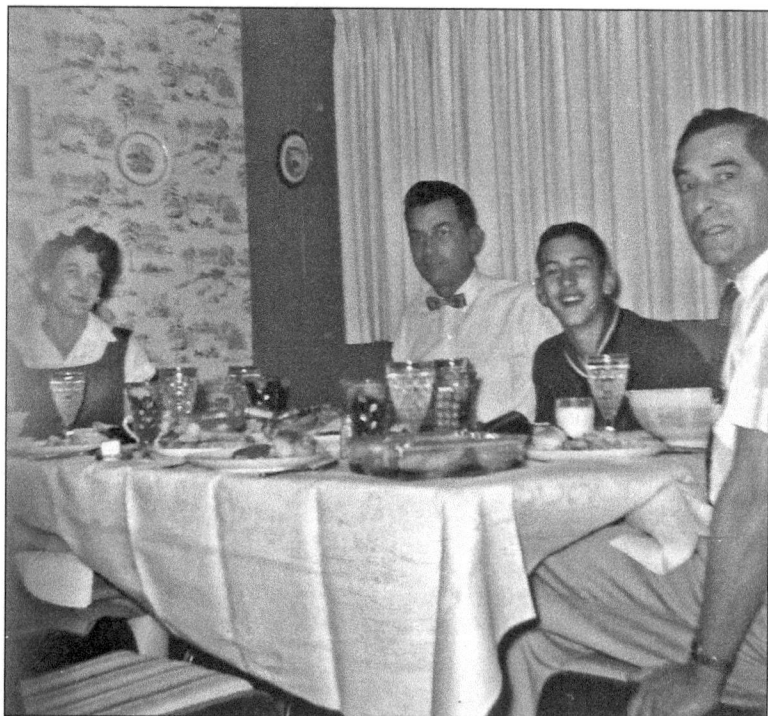

Joan Edgar sits with her sons, Mark and Larry, in their backyard in 1960. The Edgars have lived on Clayton Street in Thornton since 1956. Gerald Edgar served as a volunteer Thornton police officer in the late 1950s. (Courtesy of Joan Edgar.)

Clarence "Bud" and Rosemary Surrena were the third family to move into Thornton. The family moved to a house on Clarkson Street in February 1954. Bud Surrena served as the zone one representative for the Thornton Community Association in 1954. Here Bud Surrena is in the front yard of his house with children Patrick and Suzanne. (Courtesy of Patrick Surrena.)

57

Hazel and Jim Conley lived on Elm Place in Thornton. They owned and operated J. A. Conley and Sons Cement Contractors from 1956 to 1977. In fact, Jim Conley and Sons laid and finished all the cement work at Thornton's outdoor pool in the 1950s. Conley and Sons also did all the sidewalks at the first Wishbone restaurant at Eighty-fourth Avenue and Huron Street. J. A. Conley and Sons' business stamp can still be seen in cement work all over Thornton and surrounding areas. (Courtesy of the Conley family.)

Ivan and MaryBelle Clair moved into a Hoffman home on the corner of Downing and Eighty-ninth Avenue on September 25, 1954. This photograph shows the couple on the day they moved in. Also seen in the photograph is a 1954 Dodge that was white on the bottom, painted pink in the middle, and black on top. (Courtesy of MaryBelle Clair.)

The Miller family picked up the keys to their new Hoffman home on Lilly Drive on September 9, 1955. Pictured are Victor and Opal Miller with their daughter Sylvia. More than 50 years later, this house on Lilly Drive is still the family home. (Courtesy of the Miller family.)

Infant Michael Miller sleeps in the front yard of the Miller house in the summer of 1963 as the family dog keeps watch over the baby. In the photograph, construction crews have started grading down the hill where Highland High School was eventually built off York Street. (Courtesy of the Miller family.)

Thornton neighborhood children gather in the front yard of the Carley house in September 1957. The kids pictured are Forest "Frosty" Sterkel, Vince Carley, Ralph Forst, Scott Carley, Hugh "Skootch" Morris, Susie Sterkel, and Debbie Forst. (Courtesy of the Carley family.)

Summertime fun for Thornton kids meant riding bicycles and swimming in the pool. Neighborhood kids played outside all day, until they were called home by their moms for dinner. Pictured from left to right are childhood friends Hugh "Skootch" Morris, Scott Carley, and Vince Carley. (Courtesy of the Carley family.)

The Lone Ranger was one the heroes of the day in the 1950s. Scott Carley holds a Lone Ranger lunch box as he sits on the steps ready for school with his friend Hugh "Skootch" Morris and brother Vince Carley. (Courtesy of the Carley family.)

Brothers Robert and Jesse Scott are pictured in the front yard of their home on Eighty-ninth Avenue in 1957. The Scott family moved to Thornton in 1956. (Courtesy of Robert Scott.)

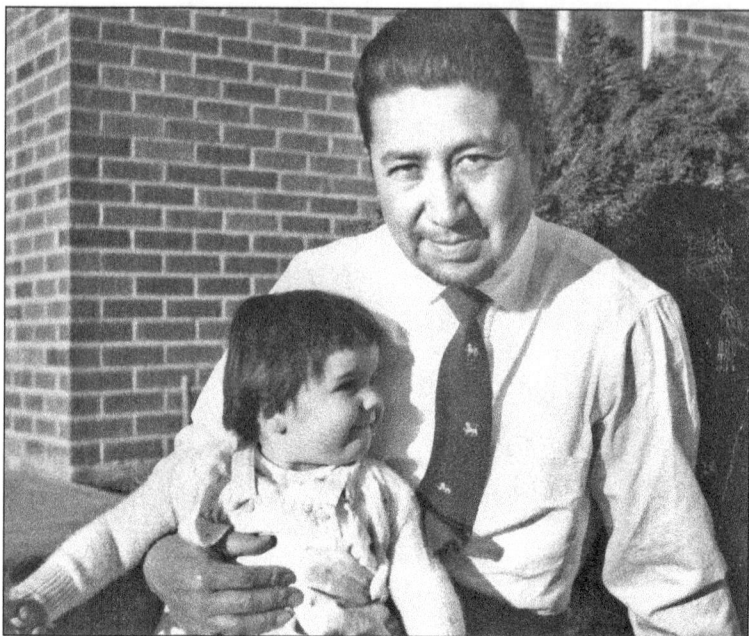

New Thornton homeowners Joseph and Ann Vigil moved into their Hoffman home on Eppinger Boulevard on May 3, 1955. Here Joe Vigil is pictured with his youngest daughter, Denise, in the late 1950s. Joe Vigil served on the Adams School District No. 1 Board of Education from 1961 to 1979. (Courtesy of the Vigil family.)

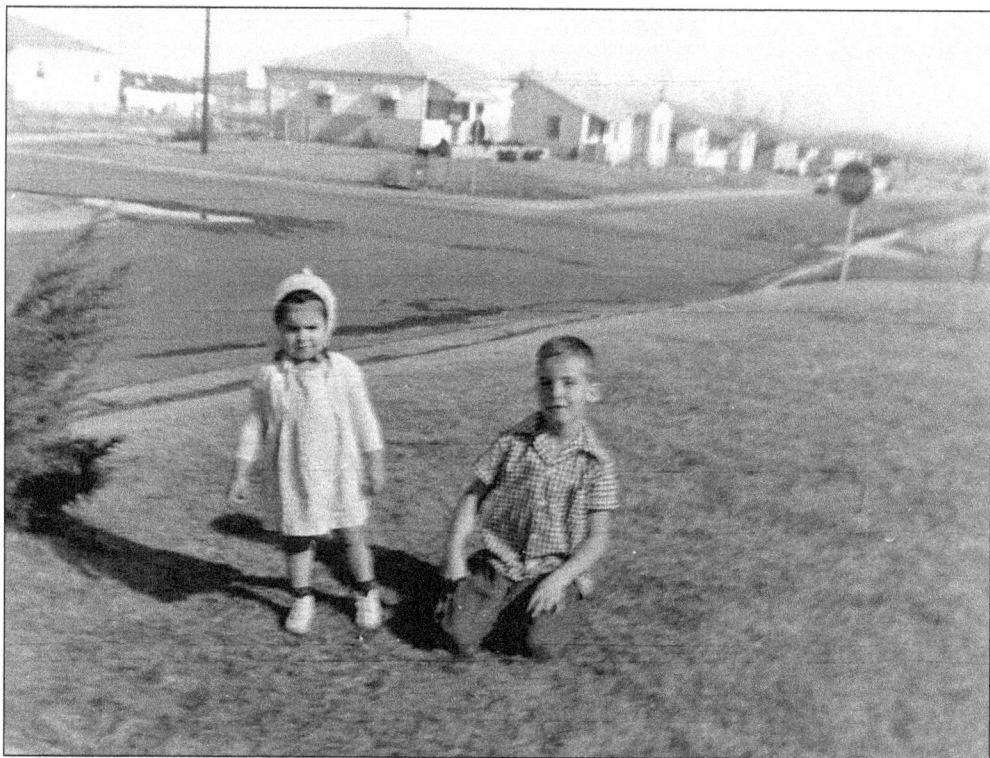

Neighborhood children Denise Vigil and Doug Cooper play together in March 1960. This photograph was taken at Carol Court and Russell Boulevard. (Courtesy of the Vigil family.)

The Petterson family moved to a Clayton house on Fir Drive in March 1955. Pete and Nadine Petterson had two children, Frank, 12, and Dianne, 10. Since there were no schools built yet in Thornton, Frank (pictured) went to Westlake School and Dianne went to the Eastlake School. Shortly after moving in, Pete Petterson found the family dog barking at a rattlesnake in their backyard. Petterson bravely caught and disposed of the rattlesnake, and the local newspaper did a story about it the next day. (Courtesy of Dianne Petterson Burchfield.)

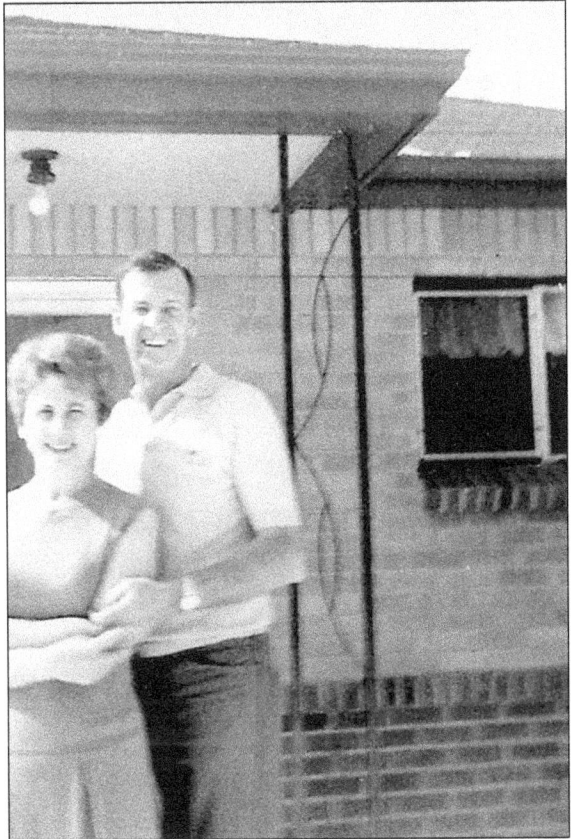

Wes and Lisa Brown moved into their Hoffman home on Nagel Drive in 1955. They had three children— Cindy, Val, and Melinda. (Courtesy of Lisa Brown.)

The Melonakis children, Matt, Angie, and Chris, play a game of football in their front yard on Fir Drive around 1956. (Courtesy of the Melonakis family.)

The Melonakis family moved to a house on Fir Drive in August 1954. George and Stella Melonakis raised their five children—Matt, Chris, Angie, Tony, and Terry—in their Hoffman home and lived there for 50 years. Here Angie and a neighbor kid are outside at the house in January 1955. (Courtesy of the Melonakis family.)

Four

EVERYONE PITCHES IN
TO BUILD
A NEW COMMUNITY

When Thornton's first citizens moved in, there was much for everyone to do. There were no gas stations, grocery stores, or even telephone service. In fact, a community phone booth was put in on a street corner so people could make calls.

However, the new citizens quickly got organized. They pulled together to offer recreation programs, raise funds for a fire truck and ambulance, and collected $1 a household to have streetlights installed.

One of the first groups to organize was the volunteer Thornton Fire Department in the spring of 1954. They formed the Thornton Fire District and began selling fire extinguishers to pay for Thornton's first fire truck, which was a 1928 Seagrave convertible engine. In 1955, the department upgraded to a 1924 American LaFrance fire truck, and land was donated to the Thornton Fire Board by developer Sam Hoffman for a fire station.

The Thornton Junior Women's Club was formed by women to improve their community. In the 1950s, they raised money for parks and constructed Thornton's first community building and a children's wading pool.

Other civic groups organized, including Thornton Kiwanis, which raised funds to purchase Thornton's first ambulance. The Thornton Lions Club and Jaycees also started.

Schools were under construction so children could attend classes close to home. Starting churches was also a priority. Homebuilder Sam Hoffman had mapped out Thornton, indicating where churches and schools should be built.

A meeting of homeowners on March 16, 1954, formed a committee to represent the people in Thornton. This group became known as the Thornton Community Association (TCA). The TCA had block leaders representing every street in Thornton.

The first proposal to create a Thornton Police Department was made in 1955. The first officers served without pay, used their own cars to patrol, and paid for their own gasoline.

By the fall of 1955, citizens formed the Thornton Recreation Association to offer recreation opportunities. Early offerings included square dancing, baseball, and swimming.

Thornton was becoming a place people were proud to call home. The next steps to becoming an official city would be historic, as two elections would soon prove.

Thornton developer Sam Hoffman (back row, third from left) stands near a sign promoting the opening of the Thornton Shopping Center to be built at Eighty-eighth Avenue and Washington Street in the 1950s. The sign states that an ultramodern shopping center will be built on the site, bringing such businesses as a bakery, shoe store, barbershop, and drugstore. (Courtesy of City of Thornton Archives.)

Thornton resident Wesley Brown was the first manager of Miller's Supermarket in the Thornton Shopping Center, starting his job in 1955. He was with Miller's for 25 years. Brown served on the Thornton Shopping Center Merchant's Association, Adams 12 Board of Education, and the Thornton Water Board. In 2006, Thornton's water plant was renamed the Wes Brown Water Treatment Plant. (Courtesy of City of Thornton Archives.)

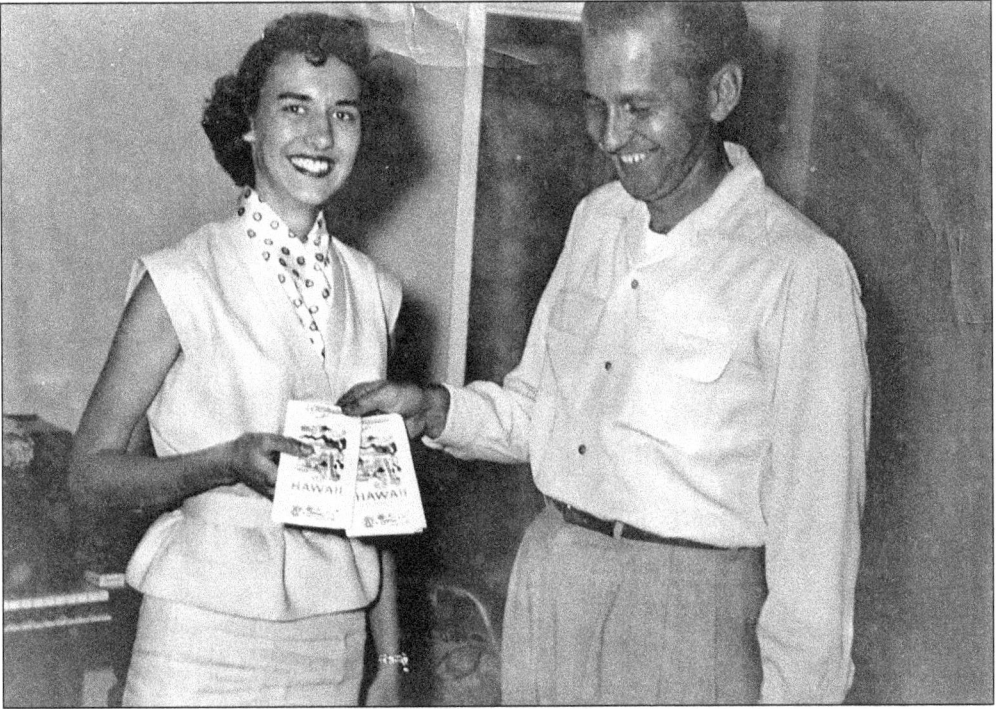

The Thornton Community Association held a raffle fund-raiser in 1954. The raffle had one lucky person winning two free airline tickets to Hawaii and hotel accommodations plus $100 in spending money. Here winner Betty O'Meara, who took a friend on the trip, accepts the tickets from TCA president Gene Hayner. (Courtesy of City of Thornton Archives.)

In 1955, the Thornton Shopping Center was under construction at Eighty-eighth Avenue and Washington Street. Thornton residents were thrilled when the shopping center opened that June. In the photograph, Woolworth's and Miller's Supermarket can be seen. Other businesses in the shopping center were Bonebrake's Toggery, Karl's Shoes, Ciancio's Restaurant, Purity Creamery, Snow White Laundry, Glendale pharmacy, Gelman Gift Shoppe, and the Northwest Utilities office. By 1956, temporary city offices were opened in the shopping center. (Courtesy of City of Thornton Archives.)

When Thornton Elementary School opened on Eppinger Boulevard, Thornton students in the Adams 12 District could now attend school close to home. The original school was built in 1955, and an east wing was added in 1956. A new school was constructed on the same site in 1978, and the original school was demolished. (Courtesy of Thornton Elementary School.)

This photograph shows students at Thornton Elementary School in the gymnasium for a special event. Thornton Elementary School principal James Cavalier stands on the stage with John Fertato. Voters approved a bond issue in 1954 to construct Thornton Elementary and Meritt Hutton Junior-Senior High School. (Courtesy of Thornton Elementary School.)

The Thornton Fire Department was started in 1954 by volunteer firemen. These volunteers worked to have Thornton citizens sign a petition to form a Thornton Fire Department by removing the area from the rural Eastlake Fire District. This was accomplished by 1955. Here are Thornton firemen at the fire station around 1956. (Photograph by Harold Palm; courtesy of the Freiberg family.)

A temporary school was constructed on Eppinger Boulevard before Thornton Elementary School was constructed. F&S Construction built the temporary building until a new school was constructed. (Courtesy of Thornton Presbyterian Church.)

The ladies of the Thornton Junior Women's Club, at one time more than 100 members strong, knew how to have fun. This photograph shows the "Fanciest Easter Bonnet Contest" held at one of their meetings in the 1960s. (Courtesy of Thornton Women's Club.)

Fashion shows sponsored by the Thornton Junior Women's Club were held annually. From parade floats to fashion shows, potlucks to costume parties and socializing, members of the Thornton Junior Women's Club have worked for five decades for the betterment of the community. Here Dorothy Marx models an outfit during a fashion show. (Courtesy of Thornton Women's Club.)

A Thornton Junior Women's Club annual tea was held in the Quonset hut Highlander building on September 11, 1962. The Thornton Junior Women's Club began publishing a city directory in the spring of 1955, listing every family in Thornton, their address, phone number, children's names, husband's occupation, and religious affiliation. The directory sold for $1 a booklet. (Courtesy of Thornton Women's Club.)

The Thornton Junior Women's Club was founded on October 6, 1954. In early years, members held annual fashion shows, created a citywide directory, and raised money for scholarships. A $1,400 wading pool was paid for by the Thornton Junior Women's Club and opened in 1958. The community building adjacent to the pool, which was constructed with funds raised by the club, was donated to the city in 1959. Here Thornton Junior Women's Club members paint and clean the community building. (Courtesy of Thornton Women's Club.)

Construction started in April 1956 on the Thornton swimming pool. Both Hoffman's construction company and the Thornton Recreation Association paid the pool construction costs. The new pool, located at Ninety-fourth Avenue and Gaylord Street, ranged from a depth of 3.5 feet to over 10 feet. The TRA officially transferred the pool and city park property to the City of Thornton in 1958. (Courtesy of City of Thornton Archives.)

Thornton children enjoy swimming on a hot summer day at the Thornton swimming pool. The pool was dedicated on August 11, 1957, when Thornton's first mayor was unexpectedly tossed into the pool with his clothes on. Later on, the pool was rented out for private events, and kids could swim for a dime for an hour after supper on summer evenings. (Courtesy of the Carley family.)

This photograph shows a Bertha-Heid Elementary School third-grade classroom in 1961. Student Ronald Greening is in the middle of the front row. Bertha-Heid School, at Ninety-first Avenue and Poze Boulevard, was opened on September 28, 1956, in the Adams School District No. 1. York Street Elementary School was built in Adams School District No. 14 in 1956. The school name was changed to York Junior High in 1957 when the school became part of Adams School District No. 1. (Courtesy of Harriet Greening.)

This is a 1962 photograph of a Clayton School class. Clayton School is in Adams School District No. 1 and is located adjacent to Bertha-Heid School. (Courtesy of the Melonakis family.)

DIRECTED TO THE FIRE COMMITTEE OF
THE CITY OF THORNTON.

12 OCTOBER 56

WE THE UNDERSIGNED WISH TO BE
ACCEPTED INTO THE CITY OF THORNTON
VOLUNTEER FIRE DEPT. WE THE UNDER-
SIGNED WILL INTURN WORK WITH THE
CITY CONCIL TO FORM A FIRE DEPT WHICH
WILL BE IN FULL ACCORD TO THE CITY'S
NEED OF LAWS TO PROTECT LIFE &
PROPERTY TO THE BEST OF OUR ABILITY.

CARL NELSON — Carl R. Nelson
AL WELTMAN —
WILBER BIGGS — Wilbert F. Biggs
RICHARD HICKS — Richard H. Hicks
HARRY SALZMAN — Harry Salzman
RUDY SALAZAR —
KEN ALLES — Ken Alles
DOUGLAS STEVENS — Douglas Stevens
VANCE UTTERBACK —
KEN FREIBERG — Kenneth J Freiberg

THANKYOU

END

This document started the Thornton Fire Department as a part of the new Thornton municipal government. On October 12, 1956, ten firemen from the volunteer department signed the handwritten document promising to work with the city council to form a city fire department. This also turned over the land, equipment, and all of the services of the fire volunteers to the city. Some early Thornton fire volunteers were Bill Williams, Bill Summers, George Teeter, Carl Kunz, Del Albee, Gordie Adams, Al Hoops, Jim Scott, Cy Leiker, John Knowles, Bill Cronin, Jim Willey, Carl Standley, Fred Larson, Bob Dawson, Greg Sheehan, Jim Hogan, George Mitze, Ted Klamann, Butch Schmidt, and Harold Valaseck. (Courtesy of the Freiberg family.)

The first Thornton fire truck was a 1928 Seagrave engine that was used from 1954 until summer 1955. At that time, the department upgraded to a 1924 American LaFrance engine, which is pictured here. Back then, all fire trucks were convertibles. Early on, the fire truck was parked at a firefighter's house in order to respond quickly to fire calls. Pictured from left to right are Charlie Grimes, Carl Nelson, and Bill Cronin. (Courtesy of the Freiberg family.)

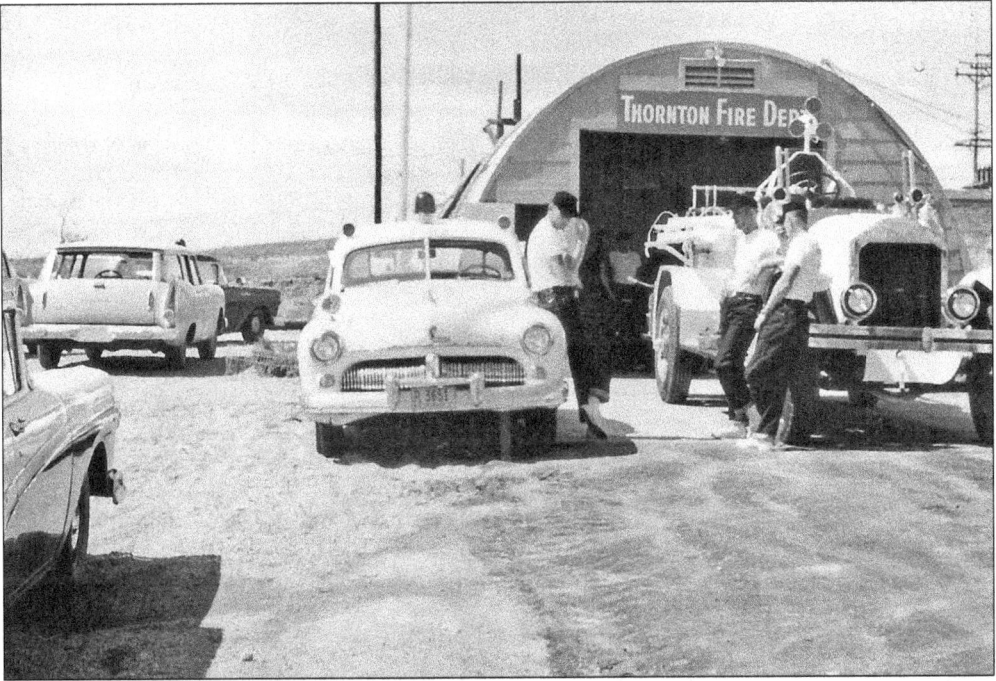

By 1955, developer Sam Hoffman donated land at Dorothy Boulevard and Nagel Street and a Quonset hut to the Thornton Fire Board for a Thornton fire station, which is pictured here. Thornton firemen stand outside the fire station in the 1950s. (Courtesy of the Freiberg family.)

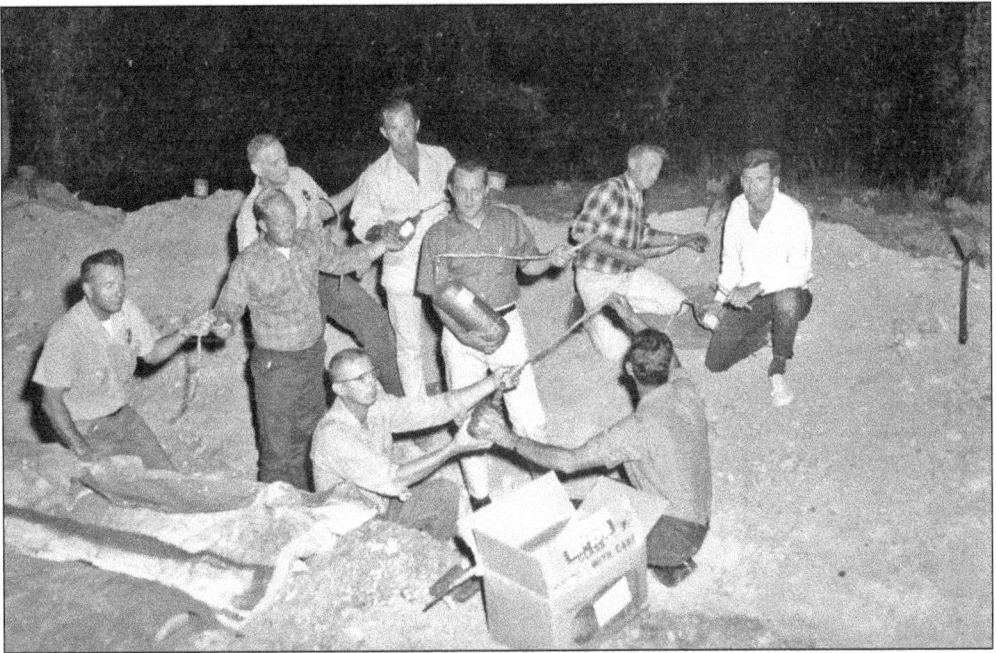

Every Independence Day in the early years of Thornton, firemen spent their holiday shooting off fireworks on the hill where Brittany Hill Restaurant sits today. Here Thornton firemen prepare to set off Fourth of July fireworks in the 1960s. In the picture are Bob Martin, Jim Scott, Jim Willey, Bob Halley, Bob Dawson, Elmer Hoops, and Ken Freiberg. (Courtesy of the Freiberg family.)

There was no shortage of dedication and leadership by early members of the Thornton Fire Department. By 1956, Carl Nelson (seen here) was appointed first fire chief of the Thornton Fire Department, which consisted of two men and a 1928 Seagrave pumper. He built a fire department from nothing and set the solid foundation for today's Thornton Fire Department. Nelson served as Thornton fire chief for 20 years. (Courtesy of the Freiberg family.)

Dorothy Nelson was the woman behind the man, as her husband Carl Nelson was Thornton fire chief for 20 years. She cooked dinners for the fire department, helped with bingo fund-raisers, and stuffed Christmas baskets. The Nelsons lived on Russell Way and had five children—Rhonda, Carl Jr., Robyn, Gunnar, and Corey. (Courtesy of the Freiberg family.)

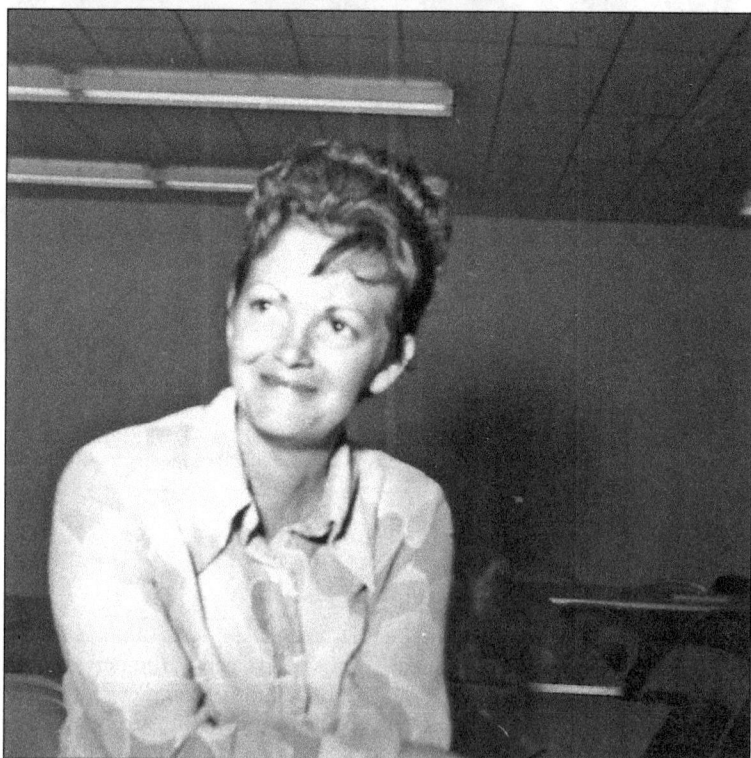

Fireman Ken Freiberg was named fire chief for the volunteer Thornton firemen. He helped found the Thornton Fire Department in 1954 and served until 1982. Freiberg was very proud to be a part of the fire department and to raise his family in Thornton. (Courtesy of the Freiberg family.)

Thornton firemen Ted Klamann and Greg Sheehan (right) gather for a fire department barbecue at a Thornton park in the late 1960s. Sheehan started as a volunteer firefighter in 1969 and came up through the ranks to be named Thornton fire chief. Sheehan was fire chief from 2000 to 2008. (Courtesy of the Freiberg family.)

Thornton firemen proved that even though they were new to the scene, they had what it took to compete in fire competitions. In their first competition in 1957, the Thornton Fire Department brought home three trophies. Pictured are Ken Freiberg (left) and Jim Scott of the Thornton Fire Department competing at a tri-county meet in Lakewood in 1961. (Courtesy of the Freiberg family.)

The newly formed Thornton Fire Department worked closely with the firemen from the North Washington Fire Protection District. For many of the early years, Thornton and North Washington firefighters practiced and competed together in regional and state fire competitions. Here they are at a state fire competition held in the 1960s. (Courtesy of the Freiberg family.)

The Thornton Fire Department held bingo fund-raisers for many years. This bingo fund-raiser was held in the Thornton Shopping Center around 1970. Some people in the picture are Mary and Ken Freiberg, Muriel and Fred Larson, Jim Scott, Cy and Nora Leiker, and Dick LaRiveria. The firefighter's wives were very involved in supporting the fire department. They even formed a Fire Flys auxiliary and competed in their own fire competition category. (Courtesy of the Freiberg family.)

Thornton firemen worked closely together and still spent some of their time off together for social events and fire competitions. Here is the Thornton firemen team competing in a state competition around 1958. Pictured from left to right are (front row) Clint Davis, Leonard Kujawski (with his daughter), Ken Freiberg, and Jim Scott; (back row) Karl Kunz, Charlie Grimes, and Jack Winslett. (Courtesy of the Freiberg family.)

The Meritt Hutton High School drill team takes the field around 1958 to fire up the home crowd to cheer on the Thornton Trojans. Meritt Hutton High School was on the east side of Washington Street near where the Five Star Stadium is today. (Courtesy of Dianne Petterson Burchfield.)

This photograph shows the Meritt Hutton High School football team in 1961. That year the team had a record of six wins and three losses, and the school basketball team had a record of seven wins and seven losses. (Courtesy of Dianne Petterson Burchfield.)

The Meritt Hutton High School class of 1961, which was the fourth graduating class at the school, poses for a photograph. The graduation ceremony was held on May 26, 1961. Meritt Hutton Junior-Senior High School opened at 810 Eppinger Boulevard in 1956 with 275 students. Meritt Hutton was a one-story brick school with a gymnasium and two wings of classrooms. (Courtesy of Dianne Petterson Burchfield.)

Going on double dates for formal school dances was popular in the 1960s, yet "steadies" usually went to dances as a single couple. After the dance, couples would celebrate by having dinner at a nice restaurant. Here Thornton students are dressed elegantly for the 1961 Meritt Hutton High School prom. Pictured from left to right are Chuck Bradbury, Carol Simmons, Dianne Petterson, and John Zengler. (Courtesy of Dianne Petterson Burchfield.)

This 1959 photograph was taken at Meritt Hutton Junior-Senior High School, which can be seen in the background. Students had to walk up stairs off Eppinger Boulevard to get to the school. In 1974, Meritt Hutton High School became a junior high when the new Thornton High School was constructed. In 1992, Thornton Middle School replaced Meritt Hutton Junior High, and the school was demolished. (Courtesy of Dianne Petterson Burchfield.)

Here is the 1961 Meritt Hutton High School baseball team. Colorado State accreditation for the school was received in 1959, and construction of the District 12 stadium was started in 1961. (Courtesy of Dianne Petterson Burchfield.)

Harriet Greening formed a Thornton Girl Scout troop in 1956. In July 1964, leaders took two troops of Thornton Girl Scouts to Washington, D.C. The adults drove station wagons and a truck with 11 girl scouts and all their gear across the country, camping along the way. Pictured here are Thornton Girl Scouts with Colorado congressman Peter Dominick in Washington, D.C. The leaders (in lighter dresses) are, in the back row from left to right, Ruth Ross, Bonnie Manning, Thelma Merrit (fourth from the right), and Harriet Greening (third from right). (Courtesy of Harriet Greening.)

By the fall of 1955, citizens had formed the Thornton Recreation Association to offer sports and recreation opportunities for adults and youth. Thornton's two championship baseball teams for one of the early years in the TRA league are pictured. Dale Sinclair's team, in the back row, was the junior division champion. The midget division champ, in the front row, was the Village Bakery team. Also pictured are, from left to right in the back row, coach Bob Legge and midget team sponsors George Grube and his wife, along with junior team sponsor Dale White and TRA athletic director Bob Frawley. (Courtesy of City of Thornton Archives.)

Thornton Festival Days always featured royalty chosen for the festivities, which included a parade and fashion show. Miss Thornton was judged in a formal pageant based on personality, talent, and beauty. The royalty for a Thornton Festival Days in 1966 included Charlene Mazzotti (right). (Courtesy of Charlene Mazzotti Moe.)

Contestants for the Miss Thornton pageant ride on a Thornton Fire Department float in a Thornton Festival Days parade in 1967. Thornton Festival Days was held each summer from 1962 until 1981 with carnivals, parades, fire department competitions, and fireworks. One of the Miss Thornton contestants pictured on the float waving to the crowd is Norma Molinaro. (Courtesy of the Freiberg family.)

The Mapleton High School freshman cheerleaders get ready to cheer for the 1961–1962 school year. Pictured from left to right are (front row) Charlene Mazzotti, Clydene Paquette, and Pattie Straface; (back row) Linda LaGuardia, Sue Martin, and Paula Piccola. (Courtesy of Charlene Mazzotti Moe.)

The Mapleton High School Falcons had real school spirit. Thornton and Welby students attended Mapleton High School together in Adams School District No. 1. Mapleton High School was located at Washington Street and Sixty-fourth Avenue. Mapleton student Charlene Mazzotti, seen here, was a cheerleader for the 1964–1965 school year. (Courtesy of Charlene Mazzotti Moe.)

Here is a Thornton Junior Women's Club float in a Thornton Days parade in the 1960s. For more than 50 years, the club's activities, social gatherings, and educational meetings have brought friends together. In the early years, women dressed in pearls and high heels and got their hair done at the beauty shop to go to their women's club meetings. (Courtesy of City of Thornton Archives.)

Construction on Thornton's Holy Cross Catholic Church started on October 13, 1957, at Eppinger Boulevard and Wigham Street. While the church was being constructed, mass was held at the Riverdale Grange Hall. The church was dedicated on September 17, 1958. A Catholic school operated at Holy Cross from 1958 to 1976. Pictured is the Rosary and Altar Society at Holy Cross Church around 1958. From left to right are Altar and Rosary Society officers Pat Pugh, Mary Beckler, Delores Mueller, Pres. Lisa Brown, and Ruth Zeylmaker. (Courtesy of Lisa Brown.)

Mountain View Lutheran Church was built at 1481 Russell Way in Thornton in March 1956. The church was founded in 1955, and services were held at Thornton Elementary School (pictured here) as the church was constructed. (Courtesy of Mountain View Lutheran Church.)

In 1954, arrangements were made to purchase land at Russell Way and Fir Drive to build a Lutheran church. Dedication services for Mountain View Lutheran Church were held on March 25, 1956. (Courtesy of Mountain View Lutheran Church.)

This is at the start of the construction for Thornton Presbyterian Church on Hoffman Way in 1956. The church's first Sunday school was in a home on Eppinger Boulevard. The first place of worship was the temporary school in District No. 12 and then in the Thornton Elementary School by October 1955. The first service was held at the Thornton Presbyterian Church on July 15, 1956. (Courtesy of Thornton Presbyterian Church.)

Fifty-three people signed the petition to the Presbytery of Denver to organize the Thornton Presbyterian Church. These people became the charter members on May 15, 1955, when the church was formally organized. (Courtesy of Thornton Presbyterian Church.)

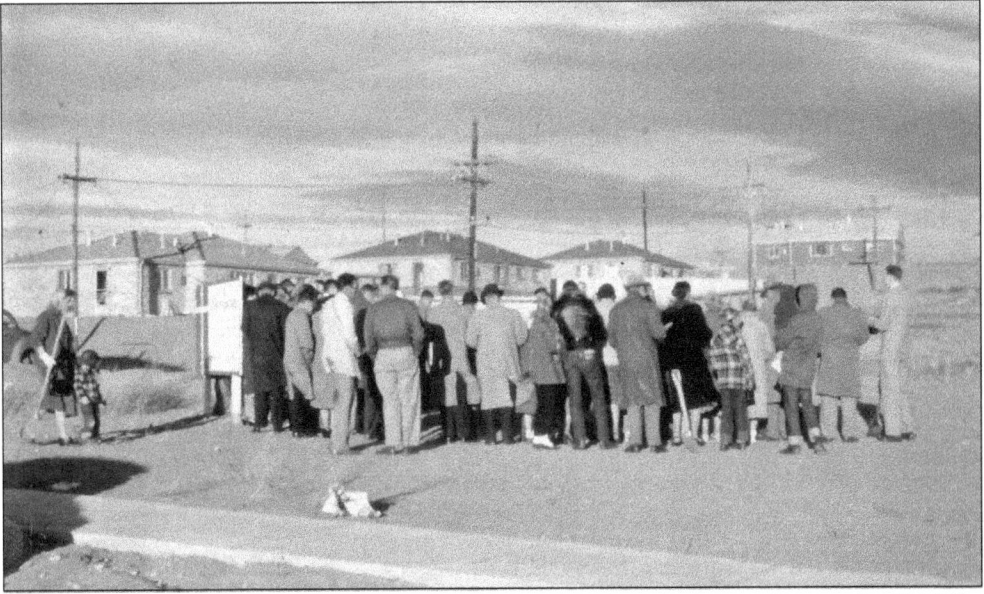

The ground-breaking for the Thornton Presbyterian Church took place on January 1, 1956. The building was constructed by that summer and the first service was held in the church on July 15, 1956. (Courtesy of Thornton Presbyterian Church.)

Three acres of land was purchased from Hoffman, Inc. to build the Thornton United Methodist Church at 8970 Hoyt Drive. The church was officially organized on April 1, 1956, with 22 charter members. On May 27, 1956, Sunday services were held at the York Street School, and the first worship service in the new church was on January 13, 1957. In 1964, the church donated 1.2 acres to the city for Lilly Park. (Courtesy of Thornton United Methodist Church.)

A ground-breaking ceremony for the Thornton Baptist Church was held on January 12, 1958. The church, built by that October, was eventually renamed Calvary Baptist Church of Thornton. (Courtesy of Calvary Baptist Church of Thornton.)

In April 1954, Calvary Baptist Church formed a Sunday school that met in a Thornton home. By that October, the church was organized and Pastor Joseph Wood was appointed. On January 5, 1955, the church moved to a house on Myrna Place for worship services. By 1957, land was purchased at Eighty-eighth Avenue and Franklin Street to construct a new church. It opened in October 1958. (Courtesy of the Carley family.)

Five

Second Time a Charm for Incorporation

By the fall of 1955, the Thornton Community Association campaigned for citizens to vote to incorporate Thornton as a city. On August 16, 1955, an incorporation election was held; however, the measure failed.

It would take another vote a year later to see Thornton officially become a city. Community leaders worked harder getting the word out the second time around. They held community meetings, went door-to-door talking to neighbors, and posted flyers about incorporation for Thornton.

The second try to incorporate Thornton was overwhelmingly successful. The tally on election night, May 26, 1956, showed that 1,280 people voted for incorporation; 165 voted against it.

The first Thornton City Council elections were on August 18, 1956. Oyer "Bill" Leary was elected Thornton's first mayor, and the first council members were Gerald Carley, Edward Gillmore, Albert Feit, John Kane, Ewell Dunn, Leonard Egelston, John Hughes, and Douglas Kinney. Also elected was treasurer Francis Anderson and clerk Bernice Holbert.

After incorporation, a police officer's desk and a city council room were set up in the firehouse's Quonset hut. A hole had to be cut in a wall to council chambers so the fire truck would still fit in the station.

The city had no money to operate at first. The city magistrate held traffic court in his home and city council worked for no pay, as did a seven-man police force and a volunteer fire department. The first city clerk stored city records under her living room couch in the beginning.

By March 1957, sources of income from business licenses and building permits started coming in. Council soon passed building codes, repaired streets, and hired paid fire and police chiefs.

By May 1958, the Thornton Post Office was opened, and voters approved a $130,000 bond for a new municipal building with police and fire stations to be opened in September 1958 on Dorothy Boulevard.

Thornton's pioneering leaders had served the community well. They would soon pass the baton to other citizens who would continue to build on the solid foundation that had been set.

A group of Thornton City Council candidates gathers during a debate in 1956 at Thornton Elementary School to discuss issues for the community. From left to right are (front row) Ed Gillmore, Bernice Holbert, Richard Berne, Lu Murray, and John Kane; (back row) Leon Egelston, Gerald Carley, Al Feit, Francis Anderson, Ken Wilson, Bill Leary, Bob Ducaj, and Doug Shockey. (Courtesy of the Carley family.)

Election commissioner Gerald Carley (left) and Al Feit, chairman of the Incorporation Election Commission, post a sign about the upcoming incorporation election in 1955. The first incorporation election for Thornton was on August 16, 1955, but failed. A second incorporation election for Thornton in May 1956 was successful. (Courtesy of the Carley family.)

Thornton leaders gathered in the basement of Tom Carrillo's house on Hoffman Way in August 1956 to wait to hear election results during the first election night in Thornton. Supporters of the Thornton City Council candidates and family members gathered to wait out the results together. Carrillo, pictured in the middle row, third from the left with the tie, would become Thornton mayor in 1972. His wife, Carmen, is pictured third from the right in the back. (Courtesy of the Carley family.)

Mayoral candidate Oyer "Bill" Leary talks about his platform while running for Thornton mayor in 1956. Mayor Leary ran on the platform of the importance to call for an immediate bond election in Thornton. The bond issue would fund fire equipment and pay to construct a combined city hall and fire department building. (Courtesy of the Carley family.)

City officials were sworn in on August 25, 1956, in front of 150 citizens who came to see the historic ceremony at Thornton Elementary School. Here the first Thornton mayor, Oyer "Bill" Leary, is sworn in. Leary defeated opponent Robert Ducaj with 782 to 447 votes on August 18, 1956. A total of 1,256 people voted in the first municipal elections. (Courtesy of the Carley family.)

This photograph shows the very first Thornton City Council meeting held at Thornton Elementary School. Mayor Oyer "Bill" Leary (standing) presides over the meeting on August 30, 1956. The first order of business was getting a $130,000 bond issue approved by voters to build a municipal building that also included a fire and police station. (Courtesy of the Carley family.)

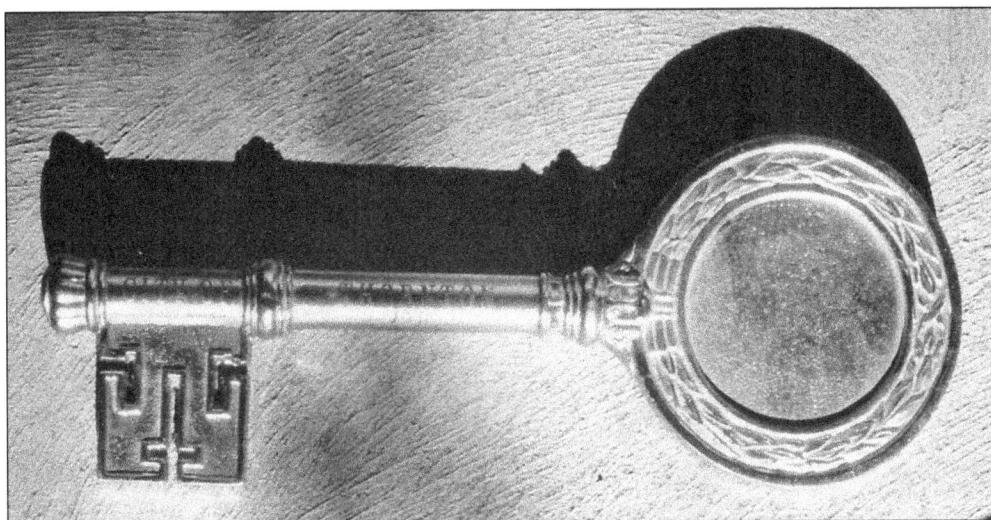

A Thornton city key was given out in 1956 to a Thornton schoolteacher who went on national television to compete on *High Finance*, a game show. Mayor Leary purchased the key from a trophy shop and asked the local woman to give the key to game show host Dennis James when she appeared on television. The mayor also sent a good-luck telegram to the Thornton teacher on August 31, 1956, at CBS studios in California. The teacher won $85,100 on the game show. Thornton's only city key is now on display at the Thornton Civic Center. The key resurfaced years later at a California garage sale and was bought by a Denver couple. (Courtesy of City of Thornton Archives.)

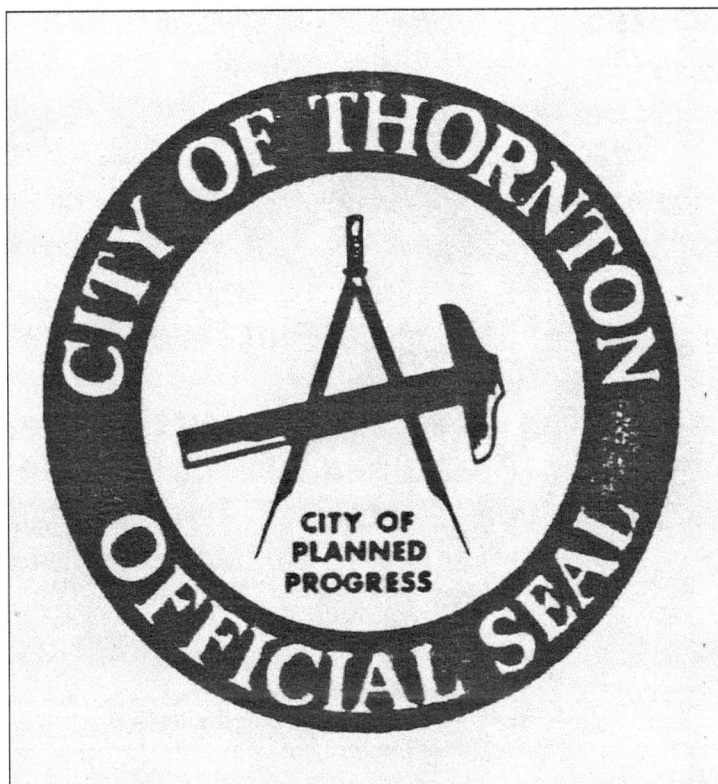

Thornton's original seal was created in 1956 by 17-year-old Mapleton High student Jim Cochran. The design was later incorporated into a city flag. The seal has the city logo, "City of Planned Progress," written on it. (Courtesy of City of Thornton Archives.)

After incorporation in 1956, the Thornton fire station's Quonset hut became the first city hall. Besides the fire department, a police officer's office and a city council meeting room were set up in the Quonset hut. Space was so limited that a hole had to be cut in the wall of the city council room so the fire truck ladder would fit in the station. (Courtesy of City of Thornton Archives.)

The goal of the Thornton Fire Department was to provide fire protection and ambulance service with a combination of volunteer and paid firemen. In 1956, when Thornton was incorporated as a city, the Thornton Fire Department became part of city operations. (Courtesy of the Freiberg family.)

96

Thornton's first police chief, Oscar Hill, was appointed in 1958. In 1957, a $12,000 annual budget was established to run the Thornton Police Department, including paying for a communications system and leasing a police car. At the time, officers worked strictly on a volunteer basis. Hill believed it to be a privilege and honor to be associated with the citizens, fellow officers, and officials who put in many long hours in the development of Thornton. (Courtesy of the Oscar H. Hill family.)

Thornton's police chief Oscar Hill stands with local boys as he gives them a reward for returning lost money they found. The boys, Gary Brovillette (left) and Roger Sumdeen had found $94 and returned it to the Thornton Police Department. (Courtesy of the Oscar H. Hill family.)

Pictured are both Thornton Fire Department and Thornton Police Department members in the late 1950s. From left to right are (front row) firemen Jim Scott and Harry Neilson with police officers Bill Morris and Gerald Edgar; (back row) firemen Doug Stevens, Leonard Kajowski, and

Jack Winslett with police officers Joe St. Onge, Vergil Jackson, Pat Sisneros, and police chief Oscar Hill. (Courtesy of the Oscar H. Hill family.)

In 1957, there were seven members of the Thornton Police Department. A few in the department were paid, but most were volunteers. Pictured from left to right are (first row) city marshal John Rogers, Chief Oscar Hill, officer Curt Kinzie, and juvenile officer Lyman Mertz; (second row) Curtis Paine and John Smiley, both volunteer Thornton deputies. (Photograph by Harold Palm; courtesy of the Oscar H. Hill family.)

Here is Thornton police chief Oscar Hill (right) with assistant chief Vergil Jackson. The Thornton Police Department started with all volunteers. Around 1957, police officers would respond to emergency calls in their own vehicles or by walking to the scene. (Courtesy of the Oscar H. Hill family.)

Ladies Auxiliary members from Thornton Veterans of Foreign Wars (VFW) Post No. 7945 volunteer their time to clean the outside of the Thornton City Hall Quonset hut. The Thornton VFW chapter was formed in November 1955. The post officially opened on June 30, 1956. (Courtesy of City of Thornton Archives.)

The original Thornton VFW Post No. 7945 hall was in an old farmhouse at 8991 Welby Road, which was renovated to add a kitchen and later a dance hall and stage. Shown here are Thornton VFW members, including Alex Lopez (right), handing out food baskets. (Courtesy of Robert Scott.)

A ground-breaking ceremony was held on January 5, 1958, for a new city hall on Dorothy Boulevard, and then construction began. Voters approved a $130,000 bond issue to fund construction of a new municipal building that opened in September 1958. This photograph shows the city hall under construction. (Courtesy of the Freiberg family.)

When the Thornton municipal building was dedicated on October 19, 1958, former governor Dan Thornton (center, with the hat) was there for the celebration. Also in attendance were Colorado governor Steve McNichols and Thornton mayor Oyer "Bill" Leary. The first permanent city hall building was located at 9471 Dorothy Boulevard, where the Thornton Senior Center is today. (Courtesy of the Carley family.)

Thornton Police Department members stand outside city hall in 1959. Pictured from left to right are (first row) assistant chief Vergil Jackson and Chief Oscar Hill; (second row) Jack Ellworth and Pat Sisneros; (third row) Donald Bishop and Joe St. Onge; (fourth row) Bill Morris. (Photograph by Benny Benham Jr.; courtesy of the Oscar H. Hill family.)

By the late 1950s, both the Thornton Fire Department and the Thornton Police Department were working together to ensure the safety of citizens. This picture shows a Thornton fire truck and a 1960 Ford Thornton police car. Thornton police chief Oscar Hill is one of the men on the scene. (Courtesy of the Oscar H. Hill family.)

In 1959–1960, the Thornton Police Department had people serving in both full-time and volunteer positions. Pictured from left to right are (first row) Lyman Mertz, a part-time juvenile officer; assistant police chief Virgil Jackson; police chief Oscar Hill; and Lu Murray, who worked as a clerk, dispatcher, and in records; (second row) Gaspie Lavoie, a reserve officer; Sgt. Curt Kinzie; officer Perry Rogers; officer Vincent DeForest; and Dick Berne, a reserve officer. (Courtesy of Vince DeForest.)

This photograph shows Mayor Oyer "Bill" Leary (white coat) with the Thornton Fire Department standing in front of the department's two new fire trucks that were delivered in 1957. Fire chief Carl Nelson is pictured next to the mayor, and Ken Freiberg, fire chief for the volunteer firemen, is on the end at right. Other firemen are Jim Scott, George Mitze, Charlie Grimes, Leonard Kujawski, John Knowles, Bill Cronin, and Clint Davis. (Courtesy of City of Thornton Archives.)

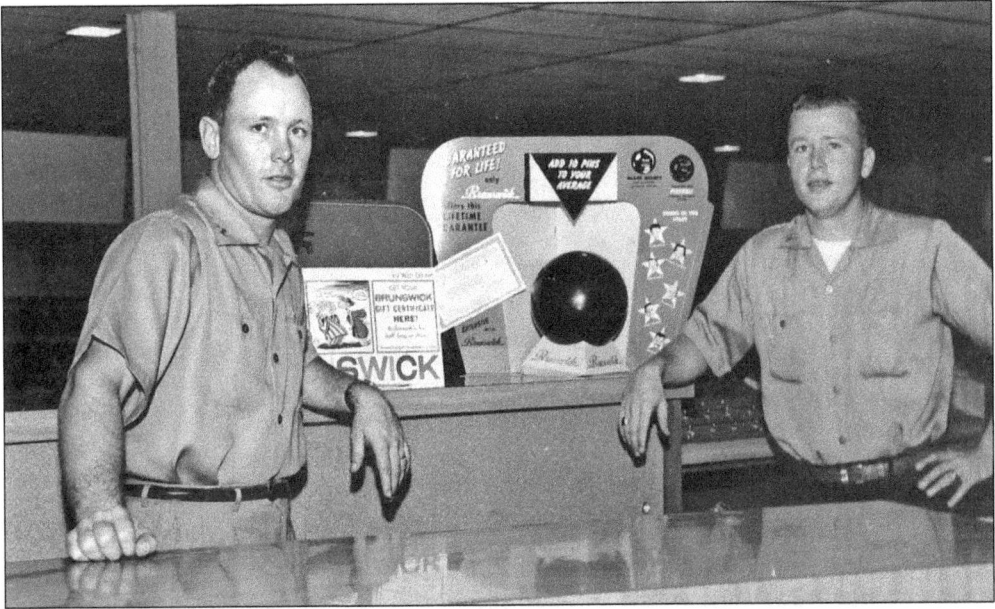

The Imperial Lanes Bowling Alley, at 900 East Eighty-eighth Avenue, was owned and operated by the Hubbell brothers, Ed and Harold. The bowling alley opened in 1957, right after setting bowling pins became automatic and the popularity of bowling leagues began to rise. (Courtesy of Ed Hubbell.)

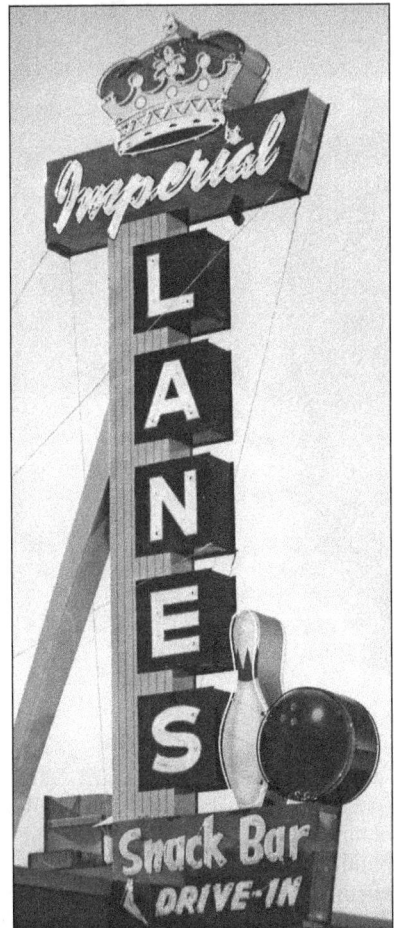

This Imperial Lanes Bowling Alley sign was outside Thornton's first bowling alley. In the late 1950s and 1960s, bowling leagues were very popular for ladies, men, and even for children on Saturday mornings. The cost of shoe rental in the 1950s was 15¢, and a game of bowling cost 45¢. (Courtesy of Ed Hubbell.)

The Mapleton High School band marches in a parade in Boulder in 1959. By 1964, Mapleton High School had a graduation class of 219 seniors. In that same year, Meritt Hutton graduated 289 seniors. (Courtesy of Albin Wagner.)

In 1960, Thornton's Civil Defense Unit was organized to promote safety in Thornton in case of air raids, Russian invasion, or nuclear attack. In 1961, Thornton City Council waived the building permit fees for construction of bomb shelters in private homes to encourage this type of construction. Pictured are members of Thornton's Civil Defense Unit, including many Thornton police officers. (Courtesy of City of Thornton Archives.)

Six

WATCHING A CITY GROW
AND SURVIVING
A TORNADO

Many significant achievements came to fruition in Thornton during the 1960s through the 1980s. In 1963, Thornton purchased the Northwest Utilities Company as its water supply. It took a citizen vote, but now Thornton leaders would control much more of the city's destiny when it came to water. The same year, a city manager form of government was adopted.

Thornton was growing and thriving. The first Thornton Festival Days was held in 1962, and in 1963, Valley View Hospital, with 50 beds, opened on Pearl Street. The North Valley Mall opened at Eighty-fourth Avenue and the Valley Highway in 1967 giving Thornton its own mall. On July 18, 1967, citizens voted to become a home rule city.

North Valley State Bank opened in the Thornton Shopping Center in February 1963 as Thornton's first bank. By November, the bank had moved into its own building on North Washington Street. This structure became the third city hall, known as the Thornton Municipal Building, in 1975.

Thornton's first recreation center and library opened in 1975. The 1976 bicentennial brought fanfare to Thornton with hot-air balloons, a rodeo, and parade as three celebrations converged: America's 200th birthday, Colorado's centennial, and Thornton's 20th.

The 1980s brought a whirlwind of activity and severe weather. Tornados touched down in Thornton on June 3, 1981. Fifty-three people were injured, cars were overturned, and houses destroyed, but fortunately there were no fatalities. Then on December 24, 1982, a blizzard hit town, leaving cars buried in snow and roads closed for days.

The Thornton Civic Center, the current city hall, was dedicated on June 26, 1983. In 1986, the Thornton Parkway interchange was built, and movie star Jane Russell returned to town, bringing Thornton full circle back to its beginning. To mark the opening of the overpass, Mayor Margaret Carpenter and Russell rode in a classic car that was the first official one to cross the roadway.

Through the years, Thornton leaders and citizens have embraced progress as the city continues to grow.

The Thornton Junior Football League formed in 1962 for boys ranging in age from 9 to 12. The league furnished uniforms and equipment and had volunteer coaches. The first president of the TJFL was Sam Guttirrez, and other organizers were Eddie Ragain, Don Coleman, and Dewey Augustine. The TJFL held its first Turkey Bowl championship game in 1962. The league still teaches boys to play football in Thornton today. (Courtesy of Thornton Junior Football League.)

In 1963, North Valley State Bank was the first bank to open in Thornton. This shows the bank when it was first located in the Thornton Shopping Center. By November 1963, North Valley State Bank moved into its new building on the east side of Washington Street. In 1974, a new North Valley Bank building was constructed at 9001 Washington Street. The bank continues to serve the Thornton community, offering checking and savings accounts, loans, and a long list of other financial services. North Valley Bank now also has branches in Broomfield and Federal Heights. (Courtesy of North Valley Bank.)

North Valley Mall, at Eighty-fourth Avenue and Washington Street, opened in August 1967. The May D&F store, with its elegant chandelier, was the first store to open. Montgomery Ward was on the east and other stores included Flag Brother's Shoes, a Hallmark store, and Pet City. Families would shop and then have lunch at Walgreen's restaurant or in the Lookout Room at May D&F. This 1979 photograph shows the entrance of the mall near the cinema. (Courtesy of the *Denver Post*.)

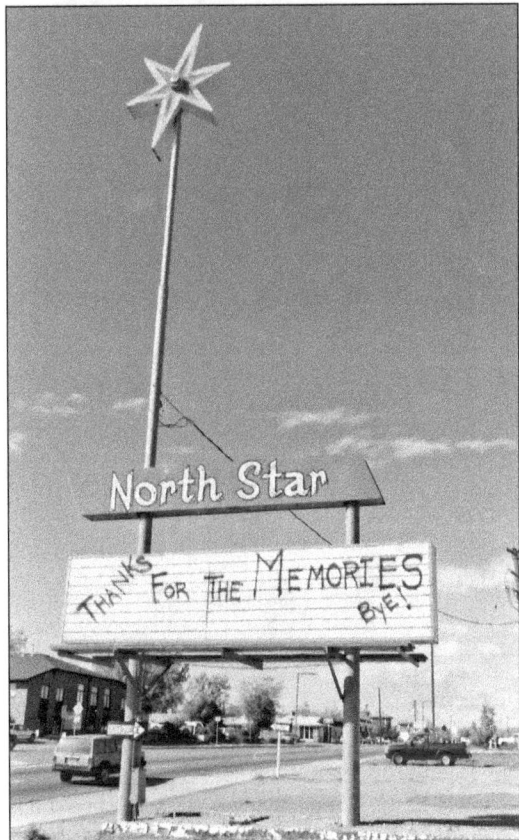

The North Star Drive-In was open in Thornton for 24 years. Families went to the drive-in for entertainment, and it was a popular hangout for teenagers. North Star opened at the northwest corner of Eighty-fourth Avenue and Interstate 25 in 1960. When it closed in 1994, a goodbye message was written on the marquee. (Courtesy of City of Thornton Archives.)

Thornton's first hospital, Valley View Community Hospital, opened on August 8, 1963. The 50-bed facility had two surgical suites, labor and delivery rooms, two nurseries, a laboratory, an X-ray department, a medical records area, a lobby, and a kitchen for patient meals. The hospital, on Pearl Street near Eighty-fourth Avenue, was started by a group of businessmen and doctors. The name was changed to Valley View Hospital and Medical Center in 1968, and by 1976 the hospital had grown to a 250-bed capacity. (Photograph by Rowena Horton; courtesy of Elaine TerAvest.)

The Chevron station and garage at Eighty-fourth Avenue and Washington Street was owned by Jim Dearing in 1960. Back then, gasoline cost 25.9¢ a gallon and was pumped by an attendant who would wash the car windows and raise the hood and check the oil and transmission fluid. A Ciancio's tavern was located next to the gas station. (Courtesy of Albert Albrandt.)

The Highland High School marching band performs for the halftime show at a Denver Broncos football game on November 19, 1972, at Mile High Stadium. The Highland marching band was organized in 1968. Highland High opened at York Street and Eighty-eighth Avenue in 1963. The first Highland High School graduating class was in 1970. The school building remains, but the name was changed to Skyview High School in 1989, when Mapleton High School was closed. (Courtesy of Harley Brown.)

A local motorcycle club, the Gravel Grimlins, had a building that was located at Eighty-eighth Avenue and York Street in Thornton. In the photograph are, from left to right, some of the members' wives, including Sonora Robbins, Mrs. Frost, unidentified, and Doris Carpenter. (Courtesy of the Miller family.)

The Thornton High School marching band takes the field to show their Trojan pride. The high school opened in 1974 on the west side of Washington Street. The name of the school has changed from Meritt Hutton High School, but the mascot has stayed the same. (Courtesy of Elaine TerAvest.)

The city's first recreation center was constructed on Eppinger Boulevard in 1975. Today the facility is called the Thornton Community Center, and it houses a gymnasium, teen center, dance studio, weight room, and preschool classrooms. (Courtesy of City of Thornton Archives.)

The colors of red, white, and blue could be seen throughout Thornton in the year 1976, which celebrated the city's 20th birthday, the 100th year for Colorado statehood, and the 200th birthday of the United States. The celebration was even more exciting as Thornton was officially designated a Bicentennial City by the American Revolution Bicentennial Administration. As part of the festivities, citizen Richard Beougher won a contest with his design for an official city flag. (Courtesy of City of Thornton Archives.)

In July 1974, the Thornton United Methodist Church was heavily damaged by fire. This photograph shows a church service being held after the fire on July 28, 1974, outside the church, which was attended by 93 people. Services were then held in the church fellowship hall until that fall when the church was repaired. (Courtesy of Thornton United Methodist Church.)

The City of Thornton moved into a new city hall building at 8992 North Washington Street in 1975. Formerly the North Valley State Bank building, city offices moved into the structure as the city grew in population and had a need to expand for more office space. The city added a second story onto the building when it became Thornton City Hall. (Courtesy of the *Denver Post*.)

Tornados touched down in Thornton on June 3, 1981, one day before the city's 25th anniversary celebration, damaging 210 houses and injuring 53 people. The path of one tornado came right down Washington Street, tearing part of the roof off the North Valley Bank building and throwing the debris across the street into the parking lot of Thornton City Hall. (Courtesy of City of Thornton Archives.)

This bird's-eye view gives a peek into the kitchen and dining area of a Thornton house after the tornado ripped the roof completely off. The refrigerator is still in place, dishes are on the table, and the phone is still hanging on the wall, but debris is strewn about. Thornton's 25th anniversary parade and celebration went on as planned the next day. (Courtesy of City of Thornton Archives.)

On December 24, 1982, a blizzard hit the metro area. People were snowed in on Christmas day, and cars were buried under snow for days. Almost two feet of snow fell during the storm. This picture was taken in the Loma Linda subdivision. (Courtesy of Elaine TerAvest.)

Since Thornton purchased the Northwest Utilities Company in 1963, Northglenn citizens paid their water bills for many years to the City of Thornton. In the 1970s, a new utilities office was opened in Northglenn at 104th Avenue and Washington Street. Secretary MaryBelle Clair, seated, is pictured with officials, including then Thornton city manager Jim Casterdale (second from right). (Courtesy of MaryBelle Clair.)

Here is Thornton's maintenance crew in the 1970s in front of what was the Thornton Public Utilities building on Dorothy Boulevard. Today the building serves as a Thornton Fire Station and the Thornton Senior Center. Ivan Clair (back row, third from right) was the superintendent of water and sewer maintenance. (Courtesy of MaryBelle Clair.)

Pictured here is a new five-story Thornton hospital, which was constructed in 1984. Humana Inc. had acquired Valley View hospital in 1978, and soon after proposed to build a new hospital. The 172-bed, Humana Hospital–Mountain View opened at Eppinger Boulevard and Grant Street on November 2, 1985. It was the first new hospital in the Denver area in 10 years. It featured a women's center and day surgery unit in addition to extensive emergency services. Brittany Hill Restaurant, built in 1983, can be seen up on the hill. (Courtesy of Elaine TerAvest.)

There were 143 graduating seniors in the Mapleton High School class of 1980, including Connie Graham, pictured on stage receiving her diploma. Connie's brother Rick Graham graduated from Mapleton High in 1975, and her sister Carol Graham also graduated from Mapleton in 1978. Commencement exercises were held on May 21, 1980, in the school gymnasium. The first graduating class for Mapleton High was in 1957. (Courtesy of the Graham family.)

Pictured here is the Skyview High School band marching in a Thornton parade. Today Mapleton Public Schools has transitioned Skyview High School into six smaller high schools. Skyview Academy High School, Global Leadership Academy, York International School, Mapleton Early College, Mapleton Expeditionary School of the Arts, and Welby New Technology High School are all part of a portfolio of school options for families. Each school falls under the umbrella of Skyview High School for athletics and performing arts but is an independent school with its own unique way of engaging students in learning. (Courtesy of City of Thornton Archives.)

Horizon High School, in Adams 12 Five Star School District, is located near 136th Avenue and Holly Street. Horizon opened in 1988. Legacy High School is another local high school educating Thornton students. (Author's collection.)

Margaret Carpenter (right) was Thornton mayor for 20 years, from 1979 to 1999. She holds the distinction of being Thornton's longest-serving mayor. Carpenter is most proud of setting a vision for the city and seeing it through during her tenure and for bringing continuity to the Thornton City Council. Here Mayor Carpenter signs a Thornton 40th anniversary book for Joan Edgar at the civic center in 1996. (Courtesy of City of Thornton Archives.)

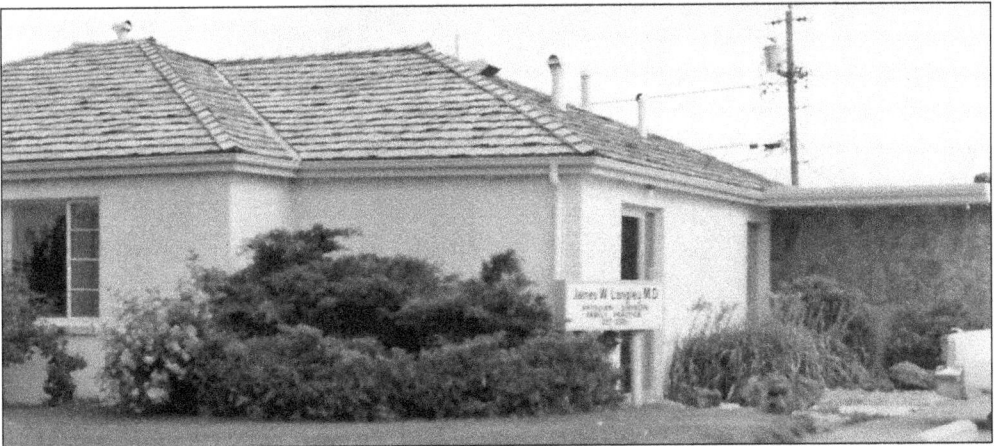

The first doctors in Thornton in the 1950s still made house calls to see sick patients, and many Thornton doctors were called out to help injured patients during ambulance calls. Pictured is the medical office of Dr. James Langley at 940 Oak Place. Dr. Langley had a medical practice in Thornton from 1958 to 1986. Other early medical facilities in Thornton included the Eighty-eighth Avenue Clinic, the North Washington Medical Building, City View Pharmacy, and Thornton Pharmacy. (Courtesy of Dr. James Langley.)

Movie star Jane Russell has a unique tie to the city. In 1953, she visited Thornton to greet people touring the Hoffman model homes. Russell returned to Thornton in 1986 for the city's 30th anniversary. She rode in a classic car with Mayor Margaret Carpenter to dedicate the Thornton Parkway overpass in August 1986. (Courtesy of City of Thornton Archives.)

The Adams County Santa Claus Workshop has been giving out toys to children of families in need at Christmastime since 1977. Pictured are Santa Shop volunteers and Santa Workshop coordinator Sarajane Anderson, who is in the foreground. Anderson has led the local effort to operate the Santa Claus Workshop for more than 30 years, and she is an original resident of Thornton since 1955. (Courtesy of Sarajane Anderson.)

Seven

HITTING A 50-YEAR MILESTONE AND STILL GOING STRONG

The city of Thornton celebrated its 50th birthday in May 2006 with a parade and community festival as past city leaders gathered for the golden anniversary. A population milestone of 100,000 people in Thornton was reached in 2003, and city borders now stretch 10 miles long, from the southern end at Eighty-fourth Avenue to the most northern part at 168th Avenue.

Thornton continues to build on the foundation from its beginnings as it grows. Today the city has a championship golf course, Thorncreek, which opened in 1992. Two years later, the Thornton Recreation Center, situated on 136 acres, was constructed. There are now two outdoor pools, and several fishing lakes that have been opened to the public.

The 64 Thornton parks enhance the natural areas in neighborhoods and add up to 792 acres of land. Parkland is diverse, with playgrounds, a skate park, and sports fields, and another 1,282 open-space acres are preserved along with 81 miles of trails.

The Thornton Police Department is 204 officers strong to serve and protect, and a new police station was constructed in 2004. The Thornton Fire Department has 91 people serving the community, and there are five fire stations in all.

City leaders continue to encourage development of diverse housing options and more business opportunities in Thornton. The community keeps on growing and evolving. Thornton even has a link beyond the atmosphere and out of this world. A business called GeoEye, formerly Space Imaging, provides satellite digital images from space. GeoEye's primary satellite operations are in Thornton, Colorado.

A legacy of service continues as organizations like the Thornton Lions and Thornton Women's Club keep on some 50 years later. Thornton pride is now celebrated at three annual festivals. Harvest Fest celebrates autumn, and Winterfest brings Santa into a lighted holiday village. The largest festival is for Thornton's birthday, Thorntonfest, when thousands come out for the day.

Perhaps what is most important today is how local festivals like Thorntonfest provide a way for neighbors to connect and build a sense of community as Thornton moves forward.

Today there are four three-story government buildings, including a police station and justice center at the Thornton Municipal Complex. Pictured here is the Thornton Civic Center, which was dedicated on June 26, 1983, at the northeast corner of Thornton Parkway and Interstate 25. Other city buildings include a Municipal Services Center at 124th Avenue and Washington Street and the City Shops at Eighty-eighth Avenue and Colorado Boulevard. (Courtesy of City of Thornton Archives.)

Thornton police officers suit up in riot gear for maneuvers on New Year's Eve in 1999. Police departments around the country had extra officers on duty to handle any potential issues due to "Y2K" computer problems when the date turned from the 1900s to the year 2000. Pictured from left to right are Thornton officers Mark Twehous, Brent Mullen, Dan Wilson, and Neal Ash. (Photograph by Jan Dexter-Blunt; courtesy of Thornton Police Department.)

Construction for the $11 million Thornton Recreation Center was approved by voters in order to see the 7,800-square-foot facility built. This photograph shows the recreation center under construction. The Thornton Recreation Center, located at 112th Avenue and Colorado Boulevard, opened in 1994 on 136 acres of land. In 2001, the facility was renamed the Margaret W. Carpenter Recreation Center to honor the former mayor. (Courtesy of City of Thornton Archives.)

Today the recreation center is one of Thornton's most popular community buildings. The center has an indoor swimming pool, fitness center and weight room, indoor running track, gymnasium, community meeting rooms, and it hosts adult and children's classes. (Courtesy of City of Thornton Archives.)

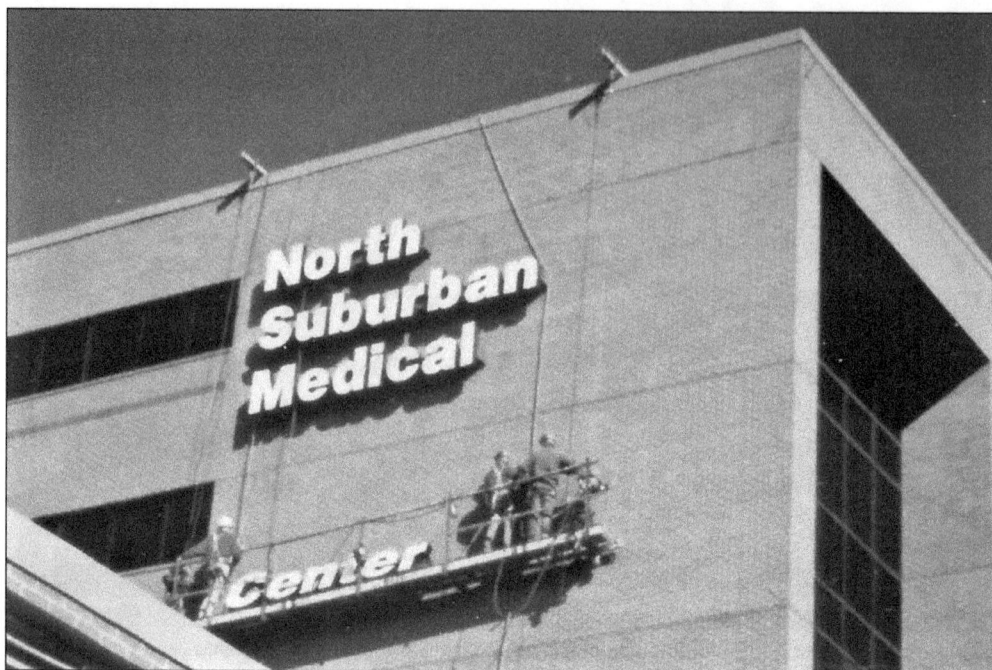

North Suburban Medical Center is Thornton's regional hospital on Grant Street off Interstate 25. The hospital received a new sign when its name was changed in 1993. In 1995, North Suburban and several other metro Denver hospitals became part of a partnership under the HealthOne name and logo, which created a network linking those hospitals. Today the medical center has a state-of-the-art emergency room, surgical center, and delivery suites for new moms. (Courtesy of Elaine TerAvest.)

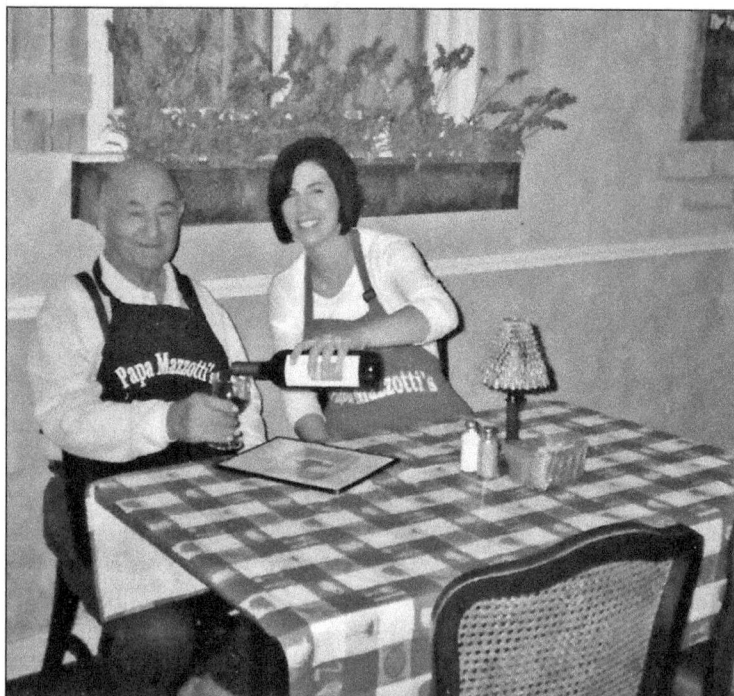

In the late 1800s, the Mazzotti's farmed land that is now in Thornton. The family name is still known around town since Papa Mazzotti's Italian Restaurant operates at 104th and Colorado Boulevard. The restaurant, which opened in 1996, is owned by Fred Mazzotti and his daughter Teri Mazzotti. Here Fred is pictured with his granddaughter Elizabeth Mazzotti Treber in the restaurant. (Courtesy of Teri Mazzotti.)

Thousands gather each May at Thorntonfest for the city's annual festival celebrating the city of Thornton's birthday. The event includes food, entertainment, a craft fair, and rides for kids. The Carpenter Recreation Center can be seen in the background. (Courtesy of City of Thornton Archives.)

Thornton celebrated its 50th anniversary in 2006 with a parade and the dedication of a new historical display at the Thornton Civic Center. The 50th celebration was tied into events throughout the year. A time capsule was also buried at the Thornton Civic Center. Here Thornton Cub Scouts participate in the city's 50th-year parade. (Courtesy of City of Thornton.)

The Radisson Graystone Castle, at 120th Avenue and Interstate 25, is one of Thornton's most unique landmarks. Opened in 1984, this hotel looks like a real castle on the outside. Today the 135-room Radisson Castle offers quality service, good food at Jester's restaurant, and banquet and catering facilities. (Author's collection.)

This image of Thornton was taken in 2002 by a satellite orbiting in space but operated from a command center in Thornton. The IKONOS satellite is owned by high-tech company GeoEye, a leading producer of satellite information. The photograph is centered on GeoEye's Thornton operations building on Grant Street near 120th Avenue. GeoEye operates Earth-imaging satellites to capture images from around the world. The business, formerly Space Imaging, opened a Thornton office in 1995. (IKONOS satellite image; courtesy of GeoEye.)

BIBLIOGRAPHY

"Bomb Shelter Fees Waived." *Thornton and South Adams Tribune*. September 14, 1961: 2.

Brenneman, Bill. "Thornton Mayor Ponders Role as Midwife to Sprawling Suburb." *Rocky Mountain News*. January 14, 1958: 14.

City of Thornton 40th Anniversary special supplement. *Northglenn-Thornton Sentinel*. May 9, 1996.

City of Thornton historical display case. "History labels." Thornton Civic Center, Thornton, CO. Established 1996 and 2006.

Daniel, Orrel A. "A Talk Concerning Municipal Incorporation." Presentation. Thornton, CO, May 6, 1955, and May 10, 1956.

———. "An orientation to the first city of Thornton newly elected mayor, city council and officers of Thornton, Colorado." Presentation. Thornton, CO, August 1956.

Eastlake Task Force. "Eastlake Master Plan." Thornton, CO: City of Thornton, December 1989.

Gavin, Tom. "Thornton Residents Equal to Problems." *Rocky Mountain News*. November 18, 1956: 24.

"Joining Thornton in celebrating 40 years of planned progress!" Thorntonfest program supplement, May 17–19, 1996. City of Thornton, 1996.

Larson, Gaye. "Thornton Slates Vote on Utility Bond Plan." *Denver Post*. March 20, 1963: 3.

Neiswonger, Debra L. *Remembering Thornton: An Oral and Social History of the City and Community of Thornton*. Thesis, University of Colorado of Denver, 1999.

"New North Valley State Bank Opens for Business." *Adams County Dispatch*. February 28, 1963: 13.

"Ranum Girl named Thornton Festival Queen." *Free Dispatch*. June 6, 1968: 1.

"Section Directors Named by Thornton Civil Defense." *Thornton and South Adams Tribune*. September 7, 1961: 1.

Thornton's First 50 Years 1956–2006. City of Thornton, 2006.

Thornton High School students, various. *Forgotten Past of Adams County*, 4 vols. Thornton, CO: Adams County School District 12, 1976–1981.

Thornton Quarterly. Thornton, CO: City of Thornton, 1990–1995.

Wagner, Albin. *Adams County, Colorado: A Centennial History 1902–2002*. Virginia Beach, VA: The Donning Company Publishers, 2002.

ACROSS AMERICA, PEOPLE ARE DISCOVERING
SOMETHING WONDERFUL. *THEIR HERITAGE.*

Arcadia Publishing is the leading local history publisher in the United States. With more than 4,000 titles in print and hundreds of new titles released every year, Arcadia has extensive specialized experience chronicling the history of communities and celebrating America's hidden stories, bringing to life the people, places, and events from the past. To discover the history of other communities across the nation, please visit:

www.arcadiapublishing.com

Customized search tools allow you to find regional history books about the town where you grew up, the cities where your friends and family live, the town where your parents met, or even that retirement spot you've been dreaming about.

www.ingramcontent.com/pod-product-compliance
Lightning Source LLC
Chambersburg PA
CBHW050602110426
42813CB00008B/2435